SAINTS & SINNERS
TALES OF LEWIS LIVES

IAIN SMITH
WITH
JOAN FORREST

SAINTS & SINNERS

TALES OF LEWIS LIVES

—

IAIN SMITH WITH JOAN FORREST

First published in 2017 by Acair Ltd, An Tosgan, Seaforth
Road, Stornoway, Isle of Lewis, Scotland HS1 2SD

www.acairbooks.com
info@acairbooks.com

Text © Iain Smith and Joan Forrest, 2017

Cover and interior design by Catriona MacIver for Acair.

A CIP catalogue record for this title is available from the
British Library

Printed by Hussar Books, Poland.

ISBN 978-0-86152-407-5

DEDICATED TO THE MEMORY
OF MY FRIEND

INA MACIVER

Acknowledgements
(in alphabetical order)

Catherine Blight;

Tom Clark;

George Cuthill;

Professor Sir Tom Devine;

Professor Joe Farrell;

Joan Forrest, my wife and my collaborator in some of this;

Ken Galloway, archivist of the Stornoway Historical Society;

My senior second cousin, Etta Graham;

Hebrides People in general and Chris and Bill Lawson
in particular;

Professor James Hunter;

Lady Macaulay of Bragar;

Iain G. MacDonald;

Seonaid MacDonald, archivist, Stornoway Museum;

Professor Matthew MacIver;

Ruairidh Maciver, my collaborator in some of this;

Dr RG Maclean;

My second cousin, Murdo Maclennan,
my collaborator in some of this;

Professor Donald Macleod;

My senior first cousin, Ann Mennie,
my collaborator in some of this;

Ian Minty;

David Newall, past Secretary of the University of Glasgow; and
the archivists of the University of Glasgow;

The Rector and the librarian archivist of the Nicolson Institute,
Stornoway;

Professor Frank Rennie of UHI;

My ex-colleague, Magnus Ross;

Scotland's People; *find my past*; and the National Archives;

Stornoway Library, notably Margaret Martin;

My brother, Professor Alasdair Smith;

My aunt, Jewel Smith;

My first cousin, Jonathan Smith;

My brother, Malcolm Smith;

My most junior but wise first cousin, Marjory Smith;

Professor Kathleen Swaim.

None of these bear any responsibility whatsoever for mistakes,
whether of fact or connotation, in my stories.

CONTENTS

INTRODUCTION

These pages are, in large part, what Professor Jim Hunter has called "illustrative case studies" and what Professor Joe Farrell has called "micro-history, a glimpse of a world which is gone."

If there is a thread to these stories, it is that they contribute something to an understanding of educational opportunity (and sometimes the lack of it) in late 19th and early 20th century Scotland. They may even have some relevance to current educational controversies.

Many of them are the stories of individuals, often highly unusual individuals. It is the atypical nature of them which is striking to me. I am slightly surprised by some readers of the individual stories who have read them as merely particularly high peaks in a generally golden landscape of talent and opportunity; so in places, notably in Chapters 4 and 5, we (i.e. I and some others) have tried – in two rather different ways – to provide a more general and measured context.

The book's main title is used entirely in a metaphorical rather than a theological sense; and is not intended to offend. Two of our characters, Alexander Macdonald and Donald Mackenzie, had church careers; and another two, John Munro and Murdo Macdonald, had that intent but died prematurely. William T Ross, Robert M MacIver and, most emphatically, Hector MacIver were not religious.

For reasons that are explained in Chapter 4 and, I like to think, have not too much to do with personal origins, I have focused in particular on the Island of Lewis; but I do say something about Scotland more generally and indeed, in Chapter 11, about comparisons with England.

For me, interest in the topics of this book began more than 60 years ago with stories my father and other family members told me. Two of these stories I pursued and cross-checked and elaborated over the last decade with great help from others, notably from my second cousin Murdo MacLellan and from my wife Joan Forrest; and they form Chapters 3 and 9.

My father (in the 1950s) told me another story of yesteryear. It went along the lines of the following:

> *An English visitor to the Highlands circa 1900 returned to his fishing lodge, saying that he had met a mad crofter. For the crofter had told the visitor that he – the crofter – had three sons. When the English visitor essayed the view that the three sons must be a great help on the croft, the crofter explained that none of the sons was free to help on his croft. For the first son was a doctor; the second was an advocate; and the third son was Secretary of State for Scotland. The Englishman had concluded that the crofter was delusional.*

> *At that point it was explained to the visitor that the crofter was entirely sane; and that the three sons of the crofter did indeed have these occupations.*

One can understand why my father, and doubtless other 20th century parents ambitious for their Scottish children, told this story. To me, a 10-yr-old, it had a (not particularly concealed) subtext: "*Scotland is a very meritocratic society; and, unlike England, has been so for some generations.*"

There is at least one problem with this story: in a literal sense, it is untrue. There is no Secretary of State for Scotland who has had a crofter father – or none that I and others have been able to trace in 45 years of trying.

It is a myth:

> *a living myth expresses something fundamental about the worldview, values, and lifestyle of the people who accept it. A myth communicates what they assume to be true about:*

- *how the world and human life really is (their worldview)*
- *how people should live in the world (their values)*
- *how people do in fact live in the world (their lifestyle)*[1]

Professor Tom Devine commented on my father's story:

I have read/heard several versions.

It is a variant of the lad o' pairts myth, such a core factor in Scotland's sense of itself in the Victorian and Edwardian era – the emotional need for identity differentiation (usually in a superior way) from England without threatening the Union, and the stock in trade of kailyard literature.

There were enough real examples, though untypical, to give credibility to the myth, especially when Carnegie grants for university study were established from the early twentieth century.

The story of Scotland's gift of an 'educated peasantry' was rehearsed at some length in the parish entries of the OSA [Old Statistical Accounts] *as early as the 1790s.*[2]

My other mentor Professor James Hunter had a rather different set of comments:

There are umpteen variations of this story.

But I'm not sure if the subtext is quite as you suggest. Underlying it, at least in the context of the middle decades of the twentieth century in much of the Highlands and Islands, is perhaps an attempt on the part of those who remained in depopulating and otherwise falling-apart communities, to put at least the beginnings of a positive spin on the seemingly interminable exodus of the young people who, in a better ordered world, might have been deploying their talents closer to home. There is much

---

1   This formulation comes from the prominent anthropologist Clifford Geertz: https://mythicamerica.wordpress.com/the-meaning-of-myth-in-the-american-context/.

2   Personal communication to Iain Smith 12 August 2015.

social, cultural and psychological complexity in all of this. I used
to puzzle quite a bit about it when, in my several years with
the Scottish Crofters Union, in crofting household after crofting
household, I'd see – in homes where parents were getting on a
bit – the graduation photographs of their children on the dresser.
'Donald's a doctor in Vancouver'; 'Mairi's a teacher in Edinburgh';
and so on and so on. There was pride in this, yes; more pride,
sadly, than in the other daughter or son, perhaps, whose photo was
nowhere to be seen but who, by virtue of still being around, on
the croft and working on a fish farm or some such, was more of a
support – albeit not usually acknowledged – to the parents than
was the doctor in Canada...

There are all sorts of further twists to this. One of the most
debilitating was the inescapable tendency – whether in the West of
Ireland or the Western Isles – to regard success as something that,
almost by definition, was attainable only somewhere else. This
too is an indicator of a pretty far gone state of affairs whereby
the person who's still around in her or his twenties is regarded
as a failure. And of course the way out, once school and higher
education was opened up to virtually everyone, was academic
attainment – witness the graduation photographs...

All sorts of other aspects of this intrigue me. What was valued
above all else was access to the professions – teaching, medicine,
the church, etc. Entrepreneurialism scarcely rated. Interestingly,
then, the most successful (in a financial sense) people around for
a time – and to some extent still – in Highland communities were
folk who were often reckoned not to have 'done well' at school.
The man with the garage business, the building business, the
haulage business or whatever, who'd never left home but who
could buy and sell any of his teacher or doctor contemporaries, was
very often the lad who'd quit school at fourteen or fifteen without
a formal qualification to his name. But he, somehow, wasn't seen
as anything like as meritorious as the doctor far away.[3]

---

3   Personal communication to Iain Smith 13 August 2015.

I return to Professor Hunter's thesis in the last chapter.

And so these chapters are about exploring what connections there might be between some Scottish educational myths and some historical reality. They are in a (very rough) chronological sequence: the main character in Chapter 1 was born in 1854 and, like the main characters in Chapters 2 and 3, was educated before the more crucial educational elements described in Chapter 4 were in place; the main character in Chapter 10 was born in 1910.

In Chapter 1 we explore a figure we stumbled upon by accident. For Joan Forrest and I were asked one day by a past colleague:

- Magnus Ross: *Why was my late grandfather persecuted by a Lewisman called JL Robertson and exiled to Scarp of all places?*

- Iain: *Good question, Magnus. Don't know. But Joan and I will look for an answer.*

Magnus's question, asked so innocently, led Joan and me to write a story of a man rightly revered in his lifetime for achievements that resonated across Scotland; but who is now but a faded footnote in a few fragile and forgotten pages. Magnus said "Well at least I now know that the man who exiled my grandfather from Shawbost to Scarp was a man of distinction."

We were a little afraid that our eventual story about Ross of Shawbost and then of Scarp, elaborated in Chapter 2 (by Joan and me), would offend our colleague. Instead he and his wife treated us to an excellent lunch. The granddad of our pal Magnus had a much tougher time in Shawbost some 100 years ago.

In Chapter 3, second cousins Murdo Maclennan and I, ourselves no youngsters, examined – with a great deal of help and encouragement from our senior second cousin Etta Graham – the story of how our black-house born[4] grand-uncle Alex Macdonald, unlike his siblings, resisted the lure of the relatively rich pickings in the late 19th century seas near Stornoway; shrugged off the absence of a school in Lewis that catered for university entrance;

---

4 pp 35–38 C Ferguson 2003 **Children of the Black-House** *Edinburgh.*

and made his way to the University of Aberdeen. Whence Africa – and Livingstone missions – called.

Chapters 4 and 5, in very different ways, are studies of how opportunities not accorded to the Robertson and Macdonald (of chapters 1 and 3) in 19th century Lewis became available about the turn of the century and certainly were quite well-established by 1910. They set a scene as to why the route to university became easier for most (but not all) of the characters in subsequent chapters.

Chapter 6 is about Professor R M MacIver, possibly the most distinguished academic ever to come from the Outer Hebrides. He infuriated some Lewis people, partly because of his acerbic insights into the Hebrides of the 1890s and then of the 1930s. His analysis of Lewis society will, to this day, cause offence to some. (He however did not cause quite as much offence as his much younger first cousin – who is in Chapter 10.)

As for Chapter 7 on Professor Donald Mackenzie, its rationale is best explained by e-mails of 2015 from and to his (USA) granddaughter, Professor Kathleen Swaim:

> Her question to me: *And why your devoted labors on my grandfather?*
>
> My answer to her: *The development of high school (i.e. secondary) education on a widespread and free basis happened in Scotland quite extensively between 1890 and 1910. In particular in 1890, the most populous island in Scotland (Lewis) had no such provision, but grew a high school by 1898 which began to send its students straight to college (i.e. university). Your grandfather Donald Mackenzie was one of the earliest of these students, one of the poorest and ultimately one of the most distinguished.*

Chapter 8 is about a dead poet from Aignish, the Nicolson Institute alumnus and dux of 1911 whose death reduced a school staffroom to tears in 1918. The contribution of the Gaelic scholar Ruairidh Maciver to this story is large. He has been over-modest in acknowledging it.

Chapter 9 is an outlier: Murdo Macdonald of Crola. He, although born as late as 1907, only ever went to a school for a day or two to sit – with success – the entrance exams for the University of Glasgow: aged about 30 in his tweed suit – and smoking roll-ups in between exams. Murdo Maclennan was again very helpful with this story.

Chapter 10 is about the outrageous (and outrageously talented) Hector MacIver. He along with some distinguished pals had a genius for alienating people, not least some of his own family. His youngest sibling died not long ago, a centenarian. She was always reticent about her slightly older brother.

Chapter 11 tries to pull some of this together.

Chapters 1, 3 and 6 to 10 have been published before in various journals; but are now revised, the revisions to some being more extensive than to others. Chapters 2, 4, 5 and 11 are new to publication. All the chapters are designed to be self-contained. So there is some repetition across chapters.

Behind these tales, there are two major intents:

1. To give an analysis of developments in Scottish education from about 1885 to 1910: an analysis familiar to some but perhaps one never written up in quite this way.

2. To tell, as my father did, some entertaining stories.

My father John Smith had very good stories. For reasons unknown to his children and to his siblings, he did not write many of them down. I hope he would have approved of my writing.

He was grateful for the educational opportunities that he had experienced. He also had some pals of somewhat similar views: Murdo Montgomery of Laxdale School, and subsequently of the Land Court of Scotland; "The Breve", George Morrison of Tolsta; "Charlie Piper" of Ballantruishal; "Dool" of Swordale; "Rusty" from Ness: who all reflected on the opportunities they had that had not been afforded to their forefathers (people who had mostly toiled in fields, hewn at rock, and chased the ling and the cod and the often elusive shoals of herring). And that is just the males of the Hebrides of 150 years or so ago. The denial of opportunity to their female ancestors and indeed to many of their female contemporaries does not bear thinking about.

All of these people of my father's circle encouraged their own children to pursue even greater educational opportunities.

My father and his mates were also comforted by the knowledge that such things would successively improve for each subsequent generation.

In that, as it turned out, they were marginally wrong.

For those of us who were school and university students in the 1950s and 1960s and who have become pensioners in the 21st century were uniquely privileged.

We did not always realise that.

I

JOHN LINDSAY ROBERTSON
A SON OF STORNOWAY

BY

IAIN SMITH & JOAN FORREST

——

J L Robertson was someone of huge talent and drive who became one of the top civil servants in Scotland. He should, some of us think, be better remembered. But there were two men of his generation, Mr Forbes and Mr Ross, who were less appreciative of him.

We start with a young boy of some ambition and some ability. One who had a father of some income.

John Lindsay Robertson was born in Stornoway in 1854, a twin boy. His mother was from Montrose, his father was a "Ship Master"[5] and/ later "Ship Owner"[6] from Stornoway and they lived in a 3-roomed house at No. 17 Kenneth Street, subsequently migrating to No. 29 in the same street, not then – or now – a locus of deprivation. So Robertson belonged to a reasonably affluent family.

He was educated at the local General Assembly School in Stornoway i.e. one of the church schools that preceded both the 1872 elementary school reforms in Scotland and the 1873 foundation of the Nicolson School in Stornoway.

By the 1871 census, he is still living at home, aged 17, but is a pupil teacher.[7] The concept of "pupil teacher" generally indicated a student staying on at school beyond the usual leaving age of 12 or 13 and possibly intending to become a certificated but non-graduate teacher via a course in a teacher training college. This was a common and comparatively well-funded route to upward mobility for males and, increasingly, for females in mid to late 19th century Scotland. Pupil teachers were paid up to £20 per year, over £2000 at 2014 prices; and many of them at 18 were then awarded bursaries (Queen's Scholarships) to attend a college free of tuition fees.[8] The importance of this, long abolished, scheme as a route to social mobility in Victorian Scotland has probably been over-looked, although Anderson's definitive work does make some considerable acknowledgement of it.[9] (In the case of one pupil teacher JR Macdonald of Lossiemouth it was a route to 10 Downing Street.)

---

5   1861 census.
6   1871 census.
7   Some authors use the style "pupil-teacher". We have chosen not to.
8   pp 55–84 M Cruickshank 1970 **History of the Training of Teachers in Scotland** *London.*
9   pp 155–158 RD Anderson 1983 **Education & Opportunity in Victorian Scotland** *Edinburgh.*

By 1871, Scottish universities were becoming increasingly rigorous in their entrance standards, and it was to be 25 years before these standards could be met by school study in Stornoway or indeed in much of rural Scotland. Macleod writes about a Stornoway Grammar School and a Stornoway Academy of the 18th century.[10] But they were long gone by the mid-19th century. However some school students, always males, used the pupil teacher scheme as a way to university entrance; and this appears to have been what Robertson did.

Robertson attended the University of Edinburgh and graduated with distinction in Arts (MA) and then in Law (LLB). So he packed a lot into the decade of the 1870s.

In 1880 (aged 26) he became an HMI (i.e. Her Majesty's Inspector of Schools) – "Her Majesty" was of course Victoria rather than Elizabeth. We know from Professor TR Bone's classic study of the Scottish school inspectorate that inspectors at the time were recruited on the basis of academic distinction rather than experience in school teaching.[11]

Much to the disgust of the main teacher union, then as now the Educational Institute of Scotland, some school inspectors of that era had no school teaching experience at all. Whether Robertson himself had briefly been a schoolteacher after graduation is uncertain; but he had at least some years of experience as the apprentice pupil teacher.

In 1888, the parish school boards[12] of Barvas, Lochs and Uig in the Island of Lewis and 10 others, all in the Highlands, were in financial difficulties, largely through the (related) issues of low attendance and poor payment of tuition fees; and they applied to the Scottish (at that time "Scotch") Education Department (SED) for special assistance. This was granted, subject to the SED having some administrative control.

---

10   pp 55–58 J MacLeod 2010 **None Dare Oppose** *Edinburgh.*
11   TR Bone 1968 **School Inspection in Scotland 1840–1966** *Edinburgh.*
12   School boards had been set up under the 1872 Education (Scotland) Act mainly to provide elementary education for 5 to 13 yr-olds (although, for some years, it was comparatively easy to leave school a little younger than 13).

It was JL Robertson who was appointed the SED administrator of the scheme; and he was promoted to acting Chief Inspector of Schools (HMCI), a position he later held on a permanent basis.

As Professor Bone describes it:

> *Robertson was a Stornoway man who, though quite young as an inspector, was admirably suited by background, temperament and energy for the responsibilities now entrusted to him. He had a shrewd understanding of the attitudes of the Highlanders, and by an unusual combination of tactfulness and audacity he brought them to accept the Department's policy. The attendance figures were raised sharply, and though strict economy was practised, educational advances were made in the schools by the broadening and brightening of the curriculum. ... it was generally admitted that he was just and sincere, and within a few years the position was becoming satisfactory again, with the return of the boards to a position of solvency."[13]*

By 1890 the three Lewis boards were indeed balancing their books and the others followed at various stages.[14] School fees in elementary (primary) board schools were abolished in 1890. Thereafter they relied, as in essence their state school successors do to this day, on a combination of government grant and local rates.

JL Robertson's main responsibilities then became those of chief district inspector for the Highlands and Islands.

Across Scotland attention had come to focus on what we now call "secondary education".

> *In 1892, the first state grants for secondary education appeared (10 years earlier than in England) and were used to build up schools in smaller towns as well as to strengthen existing ones... They formed an effective national network able to prepare both for the universities and for business careers.[15]*

---

13 p129 TR Bone 1968 **School Inspection in Scotland 1840–1966** *Edinburgh.*
14 pp 155–156 D Macdonald 1978 **Lewis: A History of the Island** *Edinburgh.*
15 p211 RD Anderson 2008 in TGK Bryce and WM Humes (Eds) **Scottish Education 3rd Edition** *Edinburgh.*

This was partly fuelled by the SED's foundation in 1888 of the Higher Leaving Certificate. It quickly became, as with remarkably few changes it remains today, the major benchmark for university entrance – and for much else. There was considerable agreement that post-elementary "higher" education should be expanded, especially for bright but poor students; but great controversy as to how.[16] Some school boards were particularly active. On the other hand, hitherto independent "higher" schools also received SED grant to expand their provision; some of them (e.g. Edinburgh Royal High School, Inverness Royal Academy, Perth Academy and indeed Paisley Grammar School – much to the chagrin of its most notorious living alumnus, one Andrew Neil) are today simply part of the state-funded system.

While both things happened and the debate in some senses dragged on as far as the 1970s, in essence the Boards won. Govan School Board was particularly prominent and proactive in this with the foundation of no less than five "higher grade" schools: Hillhead High School (founded 1885 in Cecil St) and Hyndland School (founded 1887) are still-functioning memorials to that. To this day 'GOVAN PARISH SCHOOL BOARD' is emblazoned on their surviving 19th and early 20th century buildings in large red sandstone letters. But even Govan encountered opposition because of a nearby "higher school" (Kelvinside Academy) and, where areas had several or many pre-existing "higher schools" e.g. Glasgow and especially Edinburgh, progress was slower and mired in controversy.

In the Island of Lewis, the Nicolson School had been founded in 1873 by endowment and gifts, some sadly of the most dubious of origins i.e. opium trading,[17] but was quickly to become a Board elementary (i.e. primary) school.

Building on moves initiated by his predecessor (the now somewhat maligned Forbes[18]) a new headteacher WJ Gibson

---

16 An excellent, if very dense, discussion of these issues can be found in the definitive RD Anderson 1983 **Education & Opportunity in Victorian Scotland** *Edinburgh.*
17 Chapter 12 RG Grace 2014 **Opium and Empire: the lives and careers of William Jardine and James Matheson** *Montreal.*
18 Who, as we shall see in Chapter 4, was in effect dismissed by JL Robertson.

in 1894 took over the creation and expansion of a secondary department; and bursaries "on the advice of Mr JL Robertson HMI" were awarded for the best students from rural areas.[19, 20]

Chapter 4 explains this in more detail.

Hence Donald Maclean of Bragar and Robert MacIver of Stornoway (of Chapter 6) became in 1898 the first Nicolson Institute students to go direct to university. Portree High School and Kirkwall Grammar School students began to do the same only a few years later. So across Scotland even in remote rural areas some barriers to university access were coming down: and WJ Gibson in Stornoway and JL Robertson HMCI were key players in this.

But formidable barriers (of socio-economic status and gender) remained. We know (from Maclean census data in Bragar and from Professor Robert MacIver's autobiography[21]) that the fathers Maclean and MacIver were both prosperous merchants; and this almost certainly was a factor in the educational progress of their sons. And it was no accident that the 1895 predecessor of Donald Maclean and of Robert MacIver as the first Nicolson Institute dux (Dina Macleod) had to settle for a sub-degree LLA, the delightfully titled "Lady Literate in Arts" qualification: Scottish universities began to admit women undergraduates to degree courses only in 1892, and initially the numbers were small.

JL Robertson as District Inspector was also instrumental in the Nicolson Institute acquiring and expanding its dedicated secondary building on Francis Street in 1898 and in constructing its Matheson Road infant building in 1904.

Success in secondary school provision across Scotland had however put financial pressure on government: for elementary students progressing to secondary schooling attracted a higher per capita government grant for the School Boards. So Robertson

---

19   Nicolson Institute 1973 Centenary School Magazine.
20   pp 157-158 D Macdonald 1978 **Lewis: A History of the Island** *Edinburgh*.
21   RM MacIver 1968 **As a Tale that is Told: The Autobiography of R.M. MacIver** *Chicago* and *London*.

and the Scotch Education Department in the 1900s insisted that 13/14-yr-old rural students in elementary schools passed a newly established "qualifying exam" to access the secondary education provision: this was an institution which blighted the lives of many of us until well into the 1960s. It also blighted what we call today the Primary 7 curriculum.

A perusal of the school log of Shawbost School (on the west coast of the Island of Lewis) in the 1900s suggests that Shawbost was doing poorly in "qualifying exam" results: so one can understand why Ross the Shawbost head fell out with JL Robertson; and for his pains was exiled to Scarp School for the residue of his career – a Hebridean equivalent of being sent to Siberia.

Other rural schools in Lewis were doing well in this new regime. We have tracked for example the 1900s school careers of the great, if tragic, John Munro from Knock school (son of a fisherman) and the almost equally great Murdo Murray from Back school (son of a shoemaker), both examples of rural elementary school students who accessed secondary education in the Nicolson Institute and subsequently became university graduates just before 1914.

Munro, as we shall see in Chapter 8, was a teenage prodigy in writing Miltonic verse in his second language, he was no mean Gaelic poet, he was a war hero and he was dead in France before he was 30 years old. Murray was a war poet, a school teacher, an HMI and – in his elderly years in the 1950s – a chronicler in Gaelic of his dead pal Munro. Both of them almost certainly had their paths through secondary school smoothed by JL Robertson-instituted bursaries (see Chapter 4 for more on this).

In 1912 JL Robertson was given an Honorary LL.D. by Edinburgh University.[22]

---

22 A generation or more later (1954), Professor Robert M MacIver, the Nicolson alumnus who had profited from the route to university opened up by Robertson and Gibson, received a similar honour from Edinburgh; as, a further generation or more on from that (2004), did another son of the Hebrides, Matthew MacIver, Chief Executive of the General Teaching Council for Scotland. As we shall see in Chapter 6.

In the same year, Robertson was more widely influential in Scottish social development. He was a member of the small and high-powered Dewar Committee:

> *The report presented a vivid description of the social landscape of the time and highlighted the desperate state of medical provision to the population, particularly in the rural areas of the Highlands and Islands of Scotland. The report recommended setting up a new, centrally planned provision of care that within 20 years transformed medical services to the area. This organisation, the Highlands and Islands Medical Service... acted as a working blueprint for the NHS in Scotland.*[23]

In 1915, Dr JL Robertson became HMSCI (Senior Chief Inspector i.e. the top HMI in Scotland). In 1919 he was awarded a CB (Companion of the Order of the Bath), as have been some of our more recent HMSCIs. In 1921 he retired. He subsequently gave a £5000 donation for educational purposes. From a man whose maximum career salary would have been £900 per year this was not an inconsequential sum: it is over £210,000 at 2014 prices.

> *When he died in Inverness, six years after his retirement... his popularity was clear in the extent of the activity surrounding his funeral; when his body was returned to Lewis the flags on the island were at half mast and all businesses were closed at noon. All schools throughout Lewis were closed and 'the senior boys of Nicholson [sic] Institute headed the funeral procession, which included the Lewis Pipe Band, the Brethren of the Masonic Lodge, the Provost, Magistrates and Councillors of Stornoway and members and officials of all the other public bodies'. In addition, 'there was a very large and representative attendance of the general public, including people from all parts of the island'. Sir George Macdonald, the Secretary of the Scottish Education Department, extolled his virtues and said 'Few men in our time*

---

23 http://en.wikipedia.org/wiki/Dewar_Report.

have laid their native country under so deep an obligation as he has done[24].

It is unlikely that many modern Scottish educational luminaries will receive such a send-off.

Back in the 1870s Robertson had faced barriers to university access for Hebrideans, many of which also applied elsewhere in Scotland:

1. One had to be male.

2. One generally required access to a school which was teaching to University entrance standards: the Island of Lewis, and the Hebrides more generally, had no such schools (although Robertson, and others, found a way round this).

3. One had to stay on in education beyond the age of 13: and forego the wages available to teenagers, notably in the relatively lucrative fishing industry of the time.

4. One had to pay university tuition fees; and the associated costs of travel, food and lodgings.

John Lindsay Robertson surmounted these barriers in the 1870s: he was male; he had affluent parents; he may have won bursaries; and most certainly he was talented and hard-working.

He then played a significant national role with others in lowering these barriers for subsequent generations. He should be better remembered than he is. Robertson Road in Stornoway is named after him. But not many of the good citizens of Stornoway know that.

---

24 http://ica-atom.tasglann.org.uk/index.php/dr-j-l-robertson-bequest-3;isad.

2

WILLIAM T ROSS
THE SHAWBOST HEADTEACHER

BY

Iain Smith & Joan Forrest

—

There are aspects of the early life of William Thomas Ross that are a little mysterious; but most of his adult life is well-documented. To this day, some of that archive is acquiring additions. One also gets a feel for infant mortality in Victorian times.

William Thomas Ross was born in Beauly on 6 July 1857. His father William was a draper; his mother was Margaret (née MacPherson).

By the 1871 census, the family are at 2 Church St, Inverness i.e. father William (aged 44), mother Margaret (aged 37), son William Thomas Ross (aged 14) and a 12-yr-old daughter Joan M. The first three are all recorded as "Assistant Drapers" whereas Joan M is a "Scholar". If William Thomas Ross had indeed left school at 12/13 it now becomes a bit of a mystery how and where he became a pupil teacher and then teacher. In 1872 the radical Scottish Education Act was passed. It took many years to implement, notably in rural Scotland: but created a large demand for teachers, and this just may explain some of what is to follow.

But let us take a slight digression, for reasons which will become clear.

For Catherine Banks was born about 1858 and in the 1871 census she (aged 12) is to be found in Canisbay, as is her father John aged 66 (a "boat carpenter and farmer, with 70 acres"), her mother Elizabeth (nee Bremner) aged 38 and 6 younger siblings. One sibling Alexandrina, also known as Alexina, then aged 5 and a "scholar" is to reappear in our story. Parents and all seven children were born in Canisbay, Caithness.

We know nothing of either family between 1871 and 1881, which is a pity. For somehow there was contact, some possibly amatory, some perhaps more practical, between the two families; and somehow William Thomas Ross became a teacher.

For in the April 1881 census:

i.   William Thomas Ross, aged 23, is the schoolmaster, appointed 1880, of the elementary Board school in Shawbost, Isle of Lewis – probably established in 1878 as a consequence of the 1872 Education Act. There he was to remain for more than 30 years. He is single. In the schoolhouse also live i) his sister Joan M, aged 21, who is a "schoolmistress"; and ii) a boarder, one Alexandrina Banks, aged 15, a pupil teacher from Canisbay.

ii.   Back in Canisbay still live the Banks, on an "87-acre" farm. Alexandrina obviously has vanished; as, less obviously, has Catherine. But there are still seven children at home: for John (aged 75) and Elizabeth (aged 47) have, in idle moments on the farm over the decade, added Bella (now aged 9) and Magnus (now aged 5) to their brood: H.E. Bates would have been proud of them – a Pa and Ma Larkin of Caithness.

iii.   In Dunnet, 9 miles from Canisbay, live an unmarried farmer, one John Manson with "42 acres, all arable", his sister and a house-keeper Diana Young – and the 20-yr-old[25] "domestic servant" Catherine Banks.

Later in 1881, William Thomas Ross, aged 24, is indeed again recorded as a teacher and, on 18th October, in the Free Church in Canisbay, he marries Catherine Banks, a 23-yr-old "domestic servant".

---

25   Minor discrepancies in ages should not worry us. They are common in census returns where the census return was actually filled in by an itinerant enumerator: this was the practice for 100 years or more.

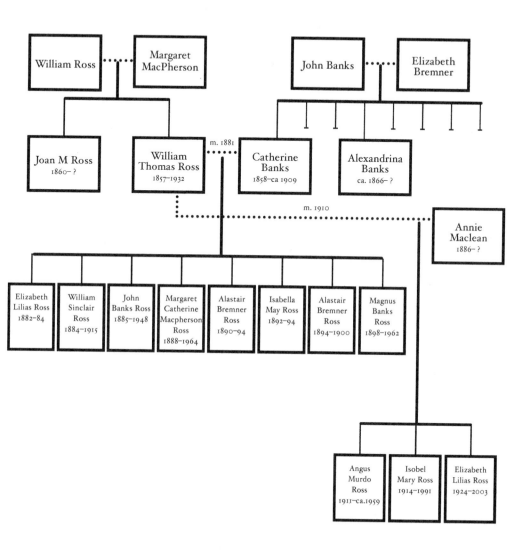

William Thomas Ross and Catherine have a daughter Elizabeth Lilias Ross on 8 August 1882;[26] but sadly she dies barely 2 years old, on 14 August 1884, of "supposed to be pneumonia".[27]

In the 1891 census, in Shawbost live William Thomas Ross (aged 34) and Catherine Ross (aged 33); three sons: the eldest William Sinclair, then a 7-yr-old "scholar", was to die in WW1 – his name is inscribed on the Stornoway war memorial and both in Shawbost[28] and in Harris;[29] John Banks Ross; and the infant Alastair, who did not survive childhood; a daughter Margt C Macpherson Ross (Margaret-Catherine MacPherson-Ross on her 1888 birth certificate); and 25-yr-old Alexina, i.e. Alexandrina Banks (sister of Catherine and "Assistant Teacher"[30]).

In the same census, but at a different address, lives a 19-yr-old Mary Morrison, a pupil teacher in Shawbost School. We knew to look for her because an autobiographical essay by her son Hector MacIver (see Chapter 10) had told us that prior to her 1895 marriage she had indeed been a pupil teacher.

Isabella May Ross is born to William Thomas Ross and Catherine on 18 August 1892; but she dies on 14 February 1894, aged 1, of a 4-day illness of "membranous croup and bronchitis".[31]

On 1 November 1894, Alastair Bremner Ross dies of a six-day illness of "tonsillitis, laryngitis and sporadic croup".[32]

On 30 December 1894 another boy is born, who is called Alastair Bremner Ross after his dead brother.[33]

In 1898, they are still in North Shawbost (William Thomas Ross as "School Master") and Magnus Banks Ross is born on 16th October to William Thomas Ross and Catherine.

26   Family records and birth certificate.
27   Death certificate viewed 6/11/2014.
28   http://pentlandroad.blogspot.co.uk/2012/04/village-memorial-north-shawbost.html.
29   http://harrismemorial.blogspot.co.uk/2008/08/scarp.html.
30   Her career progression is at least less mysterious than that of her brother-in-law.
31   Family record and birth and death certificates viewed 6/11/2014.
32   Death certificate viewed 6/11/2014.
33   Family record.

On 3rd February 1900, the second Alastair Bremner Ross dies aged 5 of a three-day "gastro-intestinal irritation and convulsions".[34]

In March 1901, they again appear in the census. Magnus is recorded as 18 months old; and has two siblings: John Banks Ross aged 15 and Margaret Macpherson Ross aged 13, both "scholars". The two teenagers are recorded as having been born in the parish of Barvas in Lewis (i.e. in Shawbost).

William Sinclair Ross, now aged 17, is not at home. He was resident in Stornoway, for in 1899 he had become a bursary-winning student of the Nicolson Institute:[35] in the 1901 census, we found him as a "scholar", one of three boarders in a 5-roomed house at 51 Keith St, Stornoway. By 1901, as we have seen, the Nicolson Institute had what we would now call a secondary department, there were now some (largely JL Robertson-initiated) bursaries available to older rural scholars and Scotland had a Higher Leaving Certificate which could lead to entrance to university or training college or directly into some professions.[36]

Our next historical trace is of the year 1905.

Surprise Find in Edinburgh[37]

This framed testimonial was gifted recently to Shawbost School by Joyce Changes from Edinburgh. The testimonial was originally presented to William Ross, the first Head Teacher of Shawbost School, by colleagues and friends in 1905 to mark his twenty five years' service to education in Lewis.

Joyce came across the frame around thirty years ago when she moved into a house in Rankeillor Street in Edinburgh. She covered the testimonial with a painting and since then it has travelled with her whenever she has moved house.

---

34   Death certificate viewed 6/11/2014.
35   Stornoway School Board minutes, August 1899.
36   pp 166 et seq. TB Dobie in TR Bone(Ed) 1967 **Studies in the History of Scottish Education 1872–1939** *London.*
37   This text is quoted courtesy of its author Iain G. MacDonald a, now retired, headteacher-successor of Ross in Shawbost; and of his present successor Ms Campbell.

23

After removing the painting from the frame recently, she decided to ask a friend, Susan Lambert, who was brought up in Stornoway and now teaches at Drummond High School in Edinburgh, to present it to Shawbost School while she was in Lewis during the Easter Holidays.

Ross served as Head Teacher in Shawbost from 1880 until 1913 and seems to have spent his last years in Edinburgh. His son Magnus[38] donated the Ross Cup for History to the school a number of years ago and it is still presented at the annual awards ceremony in the school.

The testimonial reads as follows:

'To William T Ross Esq, FEIS, Headmaster, Shawbost Public School.

We, as representing several of the Teachers of the Lewis Public Schools, and a number of former pupils and other personal friends, desire to take this opportunity of conveying to you an expression of our Respect and Esteem for you personally, and our Cordial Congratulations on your attaining your Semi-Jubilee as the Headmaster of Shawbost Public School.

We are deeply sensible of the fruitful and praiseworthy interest you have always taken in the Educational and Social Prosperity of the Lewis, and of the meritorious services you tendered to the Lewis Branch of the Educational Institute of Scotland, in the earlier years of its existence when you acted as Secretary.

We have always admired your untiring energy, zeal, and enthusiasm, in the great work of Education, while your diversified gifts, abilities and skill in imparting knowledge, are abundantly evinced by the successful careers of many of your former pupils, of whom several are now engaged in

---

38 Actually grandson.

various departments of Scholastic work, while others have achieved celebrity in other important callings at home and abroad.

As a friend you are loyal, unselfish, sympathetic and kind, and of your hospitality and goodheartedness, your many friends and professional brethren will ever have a pleasing and grateful recollection.

That you may be long spared to trim the lamp of knowledge, and advance the Educational and Social Prosperity of the Community in which you have now successfully laboured for a Quarter of a Century, is the Earnest Prayer of an everwidening circle of friends.

On their behalf we have the honour to subscribe

Ranald Macdonald J.P., F.E.I.S.

M MacIver[39]

K Mackenzie M.A.

R Ross L.R.C.P. and S

A Macdonald

Ken Macleod

Jas P Helm J.P.

L Mackinnon

P Sinclair

David Clark M.A.

Alex Macdonald C.E.

John Macleod

7 June 1905'

---

39 Probably the Mary Morrison pupil teacher of 1895: for she married a Shawbost merchant called MacIver in 1895. And was the, somewhat disapproving, mother of Hector MacIver (of Chapter 10).

On 3 Nov 1910 in Inverness, the 53-yr-old William Thomas Ross (now widowed) marries the 24-yr-old Ann Maclean of South Shawbost. On March 18 1911, Angus Murdo Ross is born in Shawbost Schoolhouse. Apparent gestation times could be short in Shawbost and – contrary to some modern belief – in much of Scotland at the time. Family memories say that Angus Murdo became a Mod gold medallist and a headteacher in Lochinver.

In April 2 1911 William Thomas Ross resides still in the Shawbost Schoolhouse, as does the 11-yr-old Magnus (at school) and Margaret Macpherson Ross (aged 23, now a "Serving Mistress School": she was eventually a primary headteacher who died in Edinburgh in 1964, aged 76).[40] But the wife of WT Ross is now of course Annie, born in the parish of Barvas; they have been married for less than a year and there is of course the infant Angus Murdo Ross. There is no sign of William Sinclair Ross or of John Banks Ross (and we did a particularly exhaustive search across Scotland for the former in 1911 census records). But we have found them in later records of a different kind.

Sergeant WILLIAM SINCLAIR ROSS[41]

Last known address in Lewis: School House Shawbost

Son of William T. Ross, F.E.I.S.,[42] and Catherine Banks Ross, of Scarp Schoolhouse, Harris.

Service unit: B Coy, 2nd Seaforth Highlanders

Service number: 9106

Date of death: 9 June 1915 at the age of 33

Killed in action

Interred: Bard Cottage Cemetery, grave VI. C. 14

---

40 Death certificate accessed 26/6/16.
41 http://facesmemorial.blogspot.co.uk/2007/07/north-shawbost-siabost-bho-tuath.html.
42 The "FEIS" is interesting. Today it is an honorary award but in the 19th century it was by examination. (p71 M Cruickshank 1970 **History of the Training of Teachers in Scotland** London.)

Village memorial: West Side, Bragar and Nicolson Institute WWı, left panel

Lewis War Memorial: Parish of Barvas, South division, panel 4

Jack Banks Ross[43]

"Jack ran away to sea when he was 14 years of age. His father was a headmaster both at Scarp and Shawbost schools.

Title: Jack Banks Ross

Date of Birth: 30-11-1885

Date of Death: 02-03-1948

Occupation: Seaman"

He married Catherine Macdonald, born in 1884 at 24 Kirkibost in Uig Lewis and died in 1946. They lived in Leith while he pursued a fishing and whaling career; and had two daughters and a son, who died aged 4.

The older daughter Catherine, born in 1914, in turn married John Collins Mackenzie, also of Kirkibost, and they settled in Lincolnshire where they had two daughters; Ruth and Mona. There are descendants in Lincolnshire to this day.

The younger daughter, Annie Christina Macdonald Banks Ross, born in 1924, was a nurse. She died at the age of 24.

In 1913, following an adverse inspectorial report on Shawbost School, William Thomas Ross, wife Annie and infant son were (forcibly) migrated to the Harris island of Scarp where Ross served the last decade of his teaching career.[44]

Two more children were born there, Isobel Mary Ross in 1914 and Elizabeth Lilias Ross in 1924.[45] Isobel Mary was probably called after her long-dead half-sister Isabella May. She eventually

---

43   http://www.hebrideanconnections.com/people/12123.
44   We know this from Shawbost school log extracts held by WTR's grandson Magnus Ross (junior).
45   On 7 April 1924 – birth certificate viewed 26 July 2016.

settled in Edinburgh and it was there in 1964 that she registered the death of her half-sister Margaret Catherine Macpherson Ross. She herself died in 1991 at Rosskeen at the age of 77.

Elizabeth Lilias Ross was certainly called after a half-sister of precisely the same name who had died in Shawbost in 1884, aged 2.

William Thomas Ross, by then retired, died in Inverness on 28 March 1932 aged 74, his death being registered by his son John (Jack) Banks Ross of Edinburgh.

An academic footnote

How did William Thomas Ross become head teacher in Shawbost? We do not know; but we do know the main mechanisms between 1872 and 1906.

The pupil teacher, as we have seen, was a feature of a teacher apprenticeship scheme of 19th century Scotland: it consistently in the late 19th century gave poor bright kids i) a moderately financially secure route to a teacher training college and to certification or ii) even directly to teacher certification; for teacher certification for bright pupil teachers with good school based mentors could be achieved by sitting the relevant exams, even without going to a teacher training college.

i)   One served from the age of 13 a 5-year apprenticeship as a pupil teacher in typically one's elementary school, followed by 2 years at, for example, the Glasgow Normal College, now the University of Strathclyde School of Education, and thus become a certificated teacher. Could William Thomas Ross have done this in the mid to late 1870s?

ii)   Could he have served a 5-year apprenticeship as a pupil teacher in Inverness and at some point, under tutelage of an Inverness headteacher, successfully taken the certificate examination as an external candidate?[46] (William Thomas Ross's "FEIS" is interesting in this respect.)

---

46   p118 M Cruickshank 1970 **History of the Training of Teachers in Scotland** *London.*

iii) Could he have simply still have proceeded to Shawbost circa 1880 as an uncertificated teacher? One would not expect an uncertificated teacher to be the head teacher and the occupant of a school house. But we cannot be sure of that, especially for a very remote rural area.

What we do know is that in 1905 Scotland had 15,000 teachers: about 8000 were in the first category; about 4000 were in the second category; and about 3000 were in the last category.[47] And the last 3000 were disproportionately in rural Scotland.

47 p135 M Cruickshank 1970 **History of the Training of Teachers in Scotland** *London.*

3

ALEXANDER MACDONALD AND A WANDERING FAMILY

BY

IAIN SMITH & MURDO MACLENNAN

———

Our maternal grand-uncle Alex was a legend in his lifetime within our family. Unlike his siblings, who chose fishing and crofting in Swordale and who married locally, he chose studies and missionary service and married into a well-travelled and well-known family.

Alexander Macdonald was born on January 12th 1879 at 18 Swordale in the Isle of Lewis, the sixth of seven children. His parents Donald (a fisherman, like his neighbours) and Maggie Macdonald, Donald's second wife, brought them up in a traditional 2-roomed "black house". Only after the 1886 Crofters Holdings (Scotland) Act gave security of tenure to crofters did it make much sense to invest in home improvements; and it took over half a century for the larger and healthier "white houses" to become common and to acquire electricity and running water. The "black house" at No 18 Swordale survived well into the 1960s.

As the historian Professor James Hunter has documented, the late 19th century was a time of considerable buoyancy in the fishing industry in Lewis[48]; and three of Alexander's brothers had by 1891 become fishermen, the father retiring from fishing and instead tending the croft. An older sister Catherine (Iain Smith's maternal grandmother and Murdo Maclennan's maternal grand aunt) went into domestic service in Glasgow, eventually marrying there and then returning to Lewis in 1910.

So by 1891 only three of the children are still at school: 8-yr-old Mary, the 12-yr-old Alexander and Murdo, aged 15. It was unusual at that time to be still in school at 15 – Murdo must have been a good "scholar" as, judging by earlier 1881 census data, had been at least two of his older brothers. The family, with a bilingual and literate father,[49] appears to have had some reverence for education – perhaps in part because their local primary school had a talented head, one Mr Morrison. Murdo was also to become a fisherman, but one who valued education – as we can tell from his subsequent family history.

Mary was to go from local fish-working (1901 census) into nursing, marry and emigrate to Canada about 1903: she spent the rest of her life there. Although recorded in family folklore as being desperately homesick in her first year in Canada, she was never again to visit Scotland (although children of hers did[50]).

48   pp 161–3 J Hunter 2000 **The Making of the Crofting Community (New Edition)** *Edinburgh.*

49   1891 census data.

50   Personal communication to us from our cousin Etta Graham.

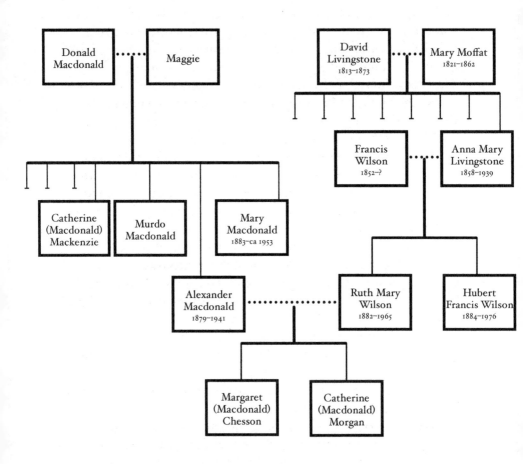

So far – apart from evidence of a high degree of literacy in the family – there is nothing unusual. The males are crofters and fishermen, with most of the family income coming from the latter occupation; the females are housewives or domestic servants; there is some migration to Glasgow and to Canada. It is a very typical pattern of late 19th century rural Lewis.

Hunter describes how the 1870s and 1880s had seen a large increase in employment of both men and women in the fishing industry in the Highlands and Islands, especially in Lewis. Many had "usually enough money to buy meat, imports of which rose steadily between the 1850s and the 1880s".[51] By the 1880s, says Hunter, families were typically spending £30 a year on imported goods compared with one-sixth of that thirty years earlier.

But then something unusual happened in the Swordale Macdonald family.

Alexander went first to the Nicolson School in Stornoway, probably about 1892 or 1893, and then on to Aberdeen Grammar School. By 29th March 1901, the 22-yr-old Alexander is recorded in the census return as a "student" i.e. at Aberdeen University.

For a crofter's son from Lewis to access secondary education in the early 1890s was rare. From the records we have traced, some other Lewis students did; but as we have seen in Chapter 1 they were almost exclusively boys from middle class backgrounds: for one needed a source of money to pay for post-primary school fees and (if from a remote rural area) for board and lodgings. If the intention was to proceed to a university degree, as in most cases it was, there was the further issue of university fees and maintenance costs. And, of course, there was the "opportunity cost" i.e. the cost of staying out of the labour market for some seven or eight years.

For girls, of whatever class, degree access to university was a "no go" area, at least until after 1892.

We know from a variety of historical sources – some national, some local – that grants and bursaries to meet the costs of secondary

---

51 p163 J Hunter 2000 **The Making of the Crofting Community (New Edition)** *Edinburgh.*

schooling and of university education became increasingly
common from the early years of the 20th century onwards; but
they were uncommon right up to the end of the 19th century
– although there were certainly bursaries available in Lewis to
attend Aberdeen Grammar School. We think that Alexander
Macdonald may have accessed one of these and may also have
obtained financial support from church sources; probably from
what in 1900 became the United Free Church. That is why, by
the 1901 census, he was a first year university student.

Alexander was a student in the University of Aberdeen from
1900 to 1904. It is possible that he obtained some additional
support over that time from the Carnegie Trust for the
Universities of Scotland (founded 1901, and an enthusiastic and
well-funded source for the payment of university tuition fees.
See Chapter 4.)

Alexander graduated and taught for a time, probably in
North Uist. But in 1908 he commenced further studies at Trinity
College Glasgow, then a divinity college of the United Free
Church of Scotland. During his time as a divinity student he held
assistantships at Inveravon United Free Church (in Moray by the
banks of the Spey) and in Greenock Gaelic United Free Church.
He was ordained by the Presbytery of Kirkcaldy in 1913.

In that year, Alexander, sponsored by the United Free Church
of Scotland mission to Africa, went to work in Chitambo (in
modern Zambia). Also in 1913 to the same mission station went
Hubert Francis Wilson and Ruth Mary Wilson, the children
of Anna Mary Livingstone: Anna Mary Livingstone was the
youngest child of the legendary David Livingstone. By then
David Livingstone was of course long dead, but various missions
had been inspired by his life, all in what are now Zambia and
Malawi. The one at Chitambo has particular historical resonance:
although Livingstone's body had been transported back for burial
in Westminster Abbey, his heart had been buried at Chitambo.

Anna Mary Livingstone, born in South Africa, had been the
product of a turbulent marriage. Anna's mother Mary Moffatt

spent much of her married life away from her husband, David Livingstone, allegedly often consoling herself with brandy; Anna's oldest brother Robert, estranged from his parents, had been killed in the American Civil War;[52] her sister Elizabeth had died at six months of age.

From age 10 onwards, Anna Mary had created a record of some considerable historical and social significance:

Ulva Cottage[53]
Hamilton
Scotland

I.

1 January 1869

Dear Mr. Anderson [sic]. *My name is Anna Mary, last-born of Mary my mother, deceased of the desert fever* [i.e. malaria] *while I was but a 'wee bairn'; I am but ten, too young to remember her voice.*

I do like your fairy tales so much – the tin soldier and the ugly, ugly duckling. I would like to go and visit you. When Papa comes home from Africa I intend to ask him to take me. I live where he began as a piecer [sic] *of cotton, threading those bales... what with the water-thrust and water-damp the Clyde is perfect for the manufacture of cloth...*

---

52 According to some sources, the parents had no idea for which side he had given his life.

53 David Livingstone's paternal ancestors were from Ulva.

II.

17 June 1871

I send you the photo of my Papa and me: his arm is about me and mine about my dolly... If you ask me he's forgotten the meaning of his own hearth; he says we're sickly and weak, bad seed, but he's the one won't kiss for bad teeth, rotten tongue...

He said bright Denmark was out of the qustion [sic]: *only dark Africa calls, where he may make himself a paradise away from this, his woven wet hell.*

III.

24 September 1874

O Hans Andersen, You will have seen from the papers how the tale has no magic ending for us, quack quack. Robert's gone, Thomas and Ossie too... Poor seed, this little mermaid never will swim.

What great, great sorry [sic] *I have had this year. I did expect Papa to take me to your Copenhagen. Instead of going the different places I fully intended with Papa, I have been obliged to take the sad journey to London to see what's left of him buried in Westminster Abbey. We had all wreaths of full white flowers to lay on his coffin; our Queen sent one too from out of her palace with deepest regrets.*[54]

So Anna's childhood had not been entirely happy; and her father was rather less of a hero to Anna than he was to Queen Victoria. She, the daughter of one European legend, had found consolation in becoming the pen-pal of the equally legendary Hans Christian Andersen.

---

54   The full correspondence is to be found chronicled in pp36–48 E Bredsdorff "Hans Andersen and Livingstone's Daughter" **Blackwoods Magazine** January 1953. Anna's letters only are in the, rather more accessible, **London Review of Books** 28 January 1993. The original letters are in the Royal Library of Copenhagen.

Perhaps it was in mind of this turbulence that Anna Mary Livingstone and husband Francis Wilson, although both essentially overseas missionaries, created a period of family stability and tranquillity in Kendal in the Lake District to rear their own two children, Hubert and Ruth.

By 1913 Anna's son Hubert Wilson was a medical graduate of the University of Glasgow. Daughter Ruth was an Edinburgh-trained nurse. As with Alexander Macdonald, they had been appointed to Chitambo by the United Free Church of Scotland. On their journey from the seaport to the mission station they had been introduced to a promising young local school boy: one Hastings Banda. Hastings Banda was subsequently a medical graduate of the University of Edinburgh, a doctor in Liverpool and the founding and (somewhat controversially) long-serving president of Malawi.

Alexander's account of his initial journey to Chitambo (in a 1930s letter to a Swordale nephew) is equally interesting:

> *When I came here in 1913 I left the train at Broken Hill and had to walk over two hundred miles and everything had to be carried on the heads of men. Each night we made a circle of poles stuck into the ground as defence against lions and other carnivores. You would think an African who had carried 60lbs on his head for 20 odd miles was tired enough. But at the end of the day when they had rested and washed they were ready to climb up a tree 50–110 ft. and cut off branches to make the pole circle.*
>
> *The journey took us 11 days but now in a motor lorry it can be done in one day.*[55]

So Alexander Macdonald the son of fisher folk/crofters from Swordale met Ruth Wilson the daughter of missionaries from Kendal.

One book paints a vivid picture of missionary life and duties in Chitambo: Hubert Wilson contributed a translation of St

---

55 Letter possessed by Murdo Maclennan.

John's Gospel to a local language production of the Bible; and generally was a leading light in the community. There is also a description of a visit (1915) by Anna Mary Livingstone. Ruth and her mother travelled to visit David Livingstone's place of death: where his heart was buried.[56]

In 1920 Ruth married "Private Alexander Macdonald": Alexander, like Hubert, had engaged in the Great War, although probably as an army chaplain rather than as an active combatant. The married couple moved between various African mission stations over the next dozen years, and raised a family of two girls.

A 2007 doctoral thesis from the University of Stellenbosch in South Africa records:

> *It was not until 1922 that the Free Church of Scotland* [sic] *made another attempt to establish a station in the Lundazi district; this was Chasefu* [in modern Zambia]*, opened in 1922 by the Rev. Donald Fraser and Alexander MacDonald, Scottish missionaries... They were both from the Livingstonia Mission.*
>
> *At the centre of the mission station, little development took place, but many remote schools were opened and supervised.*[57]

It was there that the Macdonalds spent most of the time between 1922 and 1929; they seem to have returned to the rather more developed Chitambo for their last few years in Africa.

Alexander clearly did not regard the European influence on Africa as entirely benign. In 1931 he wrote home:

> *We can grow all European vegetables and potatoes and wheat. Flour and sugar and other household supplies we buy at Broken Hill and have carried by motor lorries for an extra charge of one and three quarter pence per lb. Local produce is dear for the African and he thinks it right to try and squeeze as much out of*

56   MA Currie 2011 **Livingstone's Hospital: The Story of Chitambo** *London.*
57   V Chilenje 2007 **The Origin And Development Of The Church Of Central Africa Presbyterian (Ccap) In Zambia 1882–2004** Dissertation Presented For The Degree Of Doctor Of Theology (Ecclesiology).

the Europeans as he can. He does not see that the European is in a much better position to do the squeezing. Those who are teachers and other educated ones understand but they are so few that they have not much influence on the whole population. These things are not unknown in our own country.[58]

Alexander and Ruth left Africa in 1933. Probably they wanted their children Margaret and Catherine to have a secondary education in Scotland; and additionally Alexander was already unwell. They settled in Bunessan in Mull, where Alexander became the Church of Scotland minister for eight years. His ill-health led to his death in Edinburgh on 22nd June 1941, aged 62. The likelihood, according to eminent medical sources we have consulted, is that the liver abscess which killed him was a product of twenty years in the tropics and of his misfortune to live prior to the discovery of antibiotics.

The wanderlust traits of his family were not yet exhausted. Both daughters emigrated quite young to Canada and spent all their lives there, rearing large families. Daughter Margaret returned to Lewis on occasion to visit relatives of her father; and corresponded with Hebridean cousins well into the 21st century.

But their mother in the mid-20th century was also still migratory.

For, on 30th July 1955 Ruth MacDonald, born in November 1882 and now aged 72, sailed from Greenock to Montreal on the Empress of Scotland, being bid farewell from the Greenock quay by two of Alexander's Hebridean nieces, daughters of his long-dead sister Catherine, and by Alexander's 8-yr-old grand-nephew, a wee boy called Iain Smith.

Canada did not impress Ruth that much: she returned to Edinburgh in the early 1960s to dispense wisdom to younger generations in the tearoom of Jenner's on Princes Street; and died in Leith in 1965, aged 82. Her death made news headlines: for she

---

58 Letter possessed by Murdo Maclennan.

had been the last surviving grand-daughter of David Livingstone. Her brother Hubert survived her by over a decade.

Of the seven-sibling working class family of 18 Swordale in the 1890s, Alexander was the only one himself to use higher education as a stepping stone in life. However, in the 1920s, his brother Murdo reared a son who became a graduate teacher and headteacher; and his sister Catherine two daughters who became teachers. That, while commoner in the 1920s than it had been in the 1890s, was still relatively unusual for working class families anywhere in Scotland.

But it is Alexander, Ruth and their two children who were a particularly remarkable family. Their lives, spread across three continents, were fired by education, by religion and by migratory family genes and traditions.

4

SECONDARY EDUCATION IN LEWIS
1890–1910s

———

What we are trying to research is the story of how and why Lewis went from

• being in 1890 an island with only elementary/primary schools (one of which was the Nicolson Public School) and from where university could normally only be accessed by going to mainland schools such as Inverness Royal Academy and Aberdeen Grammar School (as we have seen with Macdonald in Chapter 3);

to

• being in 1910 and subsequently an island with a renowned secondary school (the Nicolson Institute) and feeder rural schools such that Government reports extolled what had happened as a prime example of what could be achieved more generally in Scotland.

The years following the 1872 Education Act in Scotland saw elementary (i.e. primary) schooling reasonably well established across Scotland, certainly once it became free in 1890. Problems of truancy, initially high, were largely solved.

Attention from about 1885 onwards increasingly came to focus on what we now call "secondary education"[59]. This was in part fuelled by the Scotch (sic) Education Department (SED)'s foundation in 1888 of the Higher Leaving Certificate: which quickly became, as it largely remains today, the major benchmark for university entrance. There was considerable agreement that post-elementary "higher" education should be expanded, especially for bright but poor students; but great controversy as to how.[60]

In a complex and ongoing debate, as we saw in Chapter 1, the central choice was between

- the School Boards developing their own "higher grade" (and often zero fee) provision, albeit with the SED having a regulatory function as to how and where government grant was to be spent; and

- the existing secondary provision of fee-charging "endowed schools" and "higher schools" – e.g. Kelvinside Academy, the High School of Edinburgh, Inverness Royal Academy, Perth Academy, which were mostly independent of the Boards – receiving SED grant to expand their provision.[61]

In the Island of Lewis, matters were clearer cut for there was no existing provision of "endowed higher schools".

---

59   Confusingly it was often called "higher" education until well into the 20th century.
60   Chapter 6 RD Anderson 1983 **Education & Opportunity in Victorian Scotland** *Edinburgh.*
61   p123 TR Bone 1968 **School Inspection in Scotland 1840–1966** *Edinburgh.* Professor Bone points to a third category i.e. pre-existing higher schools (e.g. the High School of Glasgow and Paisley Grammar School) which had come under Board control after 1872.

By 1890, Robertson, having taken yet another route to university as we have seen in Chapter 1, was a chief inspector: his own educational path to advancement had been eased by his having a keen intelligence and a well-off father. Robertson and others now addressed the issue of scholars who had keen intelligence but lacked well-off fathers.

[We pick up the unfolding story from archives. *Italicised* script represents direct quotes from documents; normal type represents extracts from historical documents, but not as direct quotations. And **some explanatory comments are embedded in bold type**]

1892

SEPTEMBER 5

Nicolson School

It was agreed that Mr J.L. Robertson H.M. Inspector of Schools should be asked to be present at one of the meetings of the Board in order that the Board may conver [sic] *with him and get his advice as to the staffing of this School.* (SSB)[62]

OCTOBER 3

having conferred with Mr Robertson H.M. Inspector of Schools with regard to the establishment of a department in the School for Higher Instruction unanimously resolved to advertise for an assistant master (who must be a graduate in Arts) at a salary at the rate of One hundred pounds per annum; and also for a Lady Assistant (with University qualification) for Modern Languages, advanced Music Drawing and needlework at Ninety pounds per annum. (SSB)

---

62   (SSB) = Minutes of Stornoway School Board.

DECEMBER 5

Letter received from JL Robertson HMI regarding *"the proposed establishment of a Department for Higher Instruction".* (SSB)

DECEMBER 15

"Mr John Macleod commenced duty in the Senior Department today." (LNI)[63] **This was the 'assistant master' referred to in the October 3 SSB minute.**

1893

APRIL 10

This was a special meeting of Board with JL Robertson present. Robertson on an inspection of the Nicolson School had discovered a second garden and a byre, both being run by Forbes the resident headteacher. The Board took the JLR view i.e. the byre was a health hazard to pupils; and the area of it and of the second garden was intended to be a pupil playground, not an adjunct to Forbes's garden. (SSB)

MAY 2

HMI Report:

> *I venture to suggest tentatively that the Assistant now in charge of the fourth and fifth standards should devote at least half his time to the secondary department and a large part of the remainder to the sixth standard. The recommendation on the last point is very urgent in view of the lamentable deficiency shown in the Composition, and particularly the Arithmetic, of this the highest standard, and the passport to the secondary department of the school.*
>
> *... the proper development of the institution needs very close supervision indeed. (LNI)*

---

63   (LNI) = Logbook of Nicolson Institute.

This report was probably written by Robertson. It would certainly have required his approval: for he was by now, as the archives confirm, acting Chief HMI for the district.

In 1892, a new annual grant of £60,000 had been allocated nationally within Scotland to promote secondary education.[64] That is over £7m per year at today's prices. After much debate, it had been agreed that it should be administered by county committees on which Board members, county councillors and HM Inspectorate served.

JULY 24

Resolved:

> to apply to the Ross and Cromarty County Committee [for Secondary Education] for a grant of two hundred pounds for Nicolson Public School... [and] to explain in doing so that the School is the largest and most advanced in the island... as a superior centre of Higher Education it will likely soon to have to solve the needs in this direction of a population of thirty thousand.

Also to point out that they had appointed two staff, opened new premises but needed more staff and more equipment. (SSB)

DECEMBER I

The Board had received £150 (rather than the £200 requested) from Ross and Cromarty County Committee for Secondary Education. And they had decided to use it to appoint a science teacher.

> The whole school including Secondary Department is available to scholars from all parts of the Lews, free of charge... at present there are about 10 scholars in attendance in the Secondary Department from outlying districts.

---

64 p164 T Dobie in TR Bone (Ed) 1967 **Studies in Scottish Education 1872–1939** *Edinburgh.*

All this was explained to the Board by JL Robertson, *"acting Chief HM Inspector and Chair of Ross and Cromarty County Committee"*. (SSB)[65]

So the Nicolson Public School was already, albeit on a small scale, acting as a secondary school for more than the town of Stornoway.

1894

JAN 5

All the teachers at their posts, except Headmaster – laid up for two days – Influenza. (LNI)[66]

MARCH 19

With regard to the science mastership, they reported that Mr WJ Gibson MA Rothesay Academy had been appointed.

He was additionally put in charge of Standards V and VI **[what today we would call P6 and P7]** and of the Secondary Department. (SSB)

MARCH 24

Received notice as to Leaving Certificate. Per Mr John Ross, Clerk to the School Board

'Sir... I am to state that my Lords[67] *are prepared to recognize* [sic]

---

65 I have discussed this point with a now retired Senior Chief Inspector. He, as I, takes the view that, historically and until quite recently, some members of HM Inspectorate de facto assumed direct line management functions.

66 A school student of the time, the RM MacIver of Chapter 6, takes the view that Forbes, following the untimely death of his wife, had developed an alcohol-related problem.

67 A – largely fictitious – group of Privy Councillors.

the above named school as adequately equipped for the purposes of
Article 70(e) of the Code.'

H. Craik[68]
Scotch Education Dept. (LNI)

**This was permission to enter pupils for the newly
founded Leaving Certificate, something for which explicit
SED authority was required, not least because such
students attracted a higher level of grant. As we have
noted already, the Leaving Certificate had been founded in
1888; but it was only opened up to Board schools in 1892.[69]**

MARCH 29

Notice received by Clerk as to appointment of a... Mr Gibson.
(LNI)

MAY 4

*William J Gibson MA and James Taylor have been entered in
their Lordships Register as duly Certificated teachers in this
school.* (LNI)

MAY 21

HMI Report
*Of the secondary Department it may be said that the development
is promising but very gradual indeed... the School Board are
about to re-organise and re-inforce the secondary department.*
(LNI)

**Again almost certainly written by J L Robertson. Note
the delightful phrase *"promising but very gradual indeed."*
HMIs spent more than a century writing in a code whose
meaning was clear to each other, but sometimes a touch
less clear to others.**

---

68   The first Secretary of the Scotch Education Department i.e. its top civil servant.
69   p124 TR Bone 1968 **School Inspection in Scotland 1840–1966** *Edinburgh.*

JUNE 11

Forbes was asked by the Board to tender his resignation. The only (minuted) discussion was about whether he should be *"asked"* or *"instructed"*. (SSB)

JULY 9

It was reported that Forbes had resigned. (SSB)

AUGUST 13

Gibson was appointed *"Headmaster for both Departments of the School"*. The consequent salary saving was allocated to make a Secondary English appointment. (SSB)
The main Nicolson log records neither the departure of Forbes nor the promotion of Gibson.

SEPTEMBER 21

English teacher appointment was reported to the Board: Mr McKim MA Rothesay Academy (SSB). **One notes that Gibson had come from the same school.**

OCTOBER 26

Mr Forbes gone away to take up another appointment. (LNI)

This entry – in a supplementary secondary department log – glosses over what one finds in the Stornoway School Board minutes: Forbes had been dismissed.
We shall see in subsequent archival material the opinion of JL Robertson of the effect of this transition. But there is also on record, albeit written some 70 years after the event, the opinion of RM MacIver, Nicolson school student:

> *There was nothing at school to arouse my incentive. During these years the school had been descending from bad to worse. Our Nicolson Institute had been the leading school in the outer*

islands and had acquired a fine reputation over the north of Scotland. But it was under a headteacher who had been gradually deteriorating.

Then one day

the school had been placed under a new administration. When I went to school on Monday the old headmaster had disappeared. There was a new head and there had been a general shakeup... he certainly knew his job, and once he had reformed the system everything went smoothly enough. We all came to respect him, although he did not evoke any feeling of warmth.[70]

Let us return to that in Chapter 6.

10 DECEMBER

The Board accepted a £160 County grant from Ross and Cromarty County Committee on Secondary Education (Chair: JL Robertson) and a proposal from them that £50 of it be devoted to five scholarships for students who lived at least 3 miles from Nicolson School. (SSB)

The importance of these bursaries – each worth about £1100 per year at 2014 prices – for rural access to the Nicolson is emphasised by Macdonald.[71]

1895

MAY 7

HMI Report:[72]

Since last inspection this important school has been very thoroughly organised, and the staff in the higher department has been greatly reinforced by the appointment of well qualified assistants. The school is now established and equipped as a centre

---

70   pp17–18 RM MacIver 1968 **As a Tale That Is Told** *Chicago.*
71   pp157–8 D Macdonald 1978 **Lewis: A History of the Island** *Edinburgh.*
72   Probably by JL Robertson.

*for secondary education for the whole island of Lewis and in
this respect it is specially subsidised by the County Committee
on Secondary Education and by the Trust for Education in the
Highlands and Islands. The main aim is presentation for the
Leaving Certificate.*

*The declared function of the school as the chief secondary centre
for the island is gradually being realised, so far as an influx of
selected pupils from rural schools into the higher department
is evidence that the classes and standing of the school are being
admitted outside the immediate area. (10 staff, 4 of them pupil
teachers.)*

The same minute records that Donaldina Macleod was the
first dux of the school. (LNI) **She subsequently qualified, as
we have already noted, as "Lady Literate in Arts".**

August 27

There is a named list of pupils having achieved Leaving
Certificate passes. The names include: Donaldina Macleod
(Lower English; Lower mathematics); Robert M MacIver
(Higher arithmetic; Lower French); Alexander Macdonald
(Lower arithmetic) (LNI).

**The first two were school duxes – in 1895 and 1898
respectively; the last is possibly Alexander Macdonald
of Swordale, one of the last pupils (as we have seen in
Chapter 3) to go to university via a combination of the
Nicolson School and of Aberdeen Grammar School.**

1896

March 16

The Secondary Department transfers to the (newly acquired)
Free Church School Building. (LNI)

**This acquisition had not been without legal difficulties –
JL Robertson played a key role in resolving them.**

MAY 11

HMI Report:

This important school continues to make very good progress.

14 staff
Medal for English: Robert M MacIver (LNI)

1897

APRIL 22

The specific subjects were inspected yesterday and today by JL Robertson Esq. (LNI)

JUNE 13

The Leaving Certificate was being undertaken in several subjects, notably:

	Lower	Higher	Hons
Maths	26	5	1
English	22	13	4
French	20	6	2

The Leaving Certificate was introduced in 1888. "Highers" were quickly accepted by universities and "Lowers" by certain professions e.g. as entry to banking. The category of "Higher" lasts to this day, largely unchanged – and was a brilliant advance. The category of "Lower" was abandoned in 1962, to be transformed into Ordinary Grade (a considerable success story), then into Standard Grade, and now into National qualifications.[73]

---

73 p 156 T Dobie in TR Bone (Ed) 1967 **Studies in Scottish Education 1872–1939** *Edinburgh.*

The category of "Honours" was quickly abandoned. An intended 1888 function had been similar to one in 1998 for the "Advanced Higher" i.e. to give accelerated or "fast track" entry to specialist university study. This intent of the late 19th century was as unrealised as that of the late 20th century.

JULY 2

Dux Medal – Donald Maclean (from Bragar).[74] (LNI) **Bragar lies not just outside the town by some 15 miles but outside the Parish of Stornoway. Maclean lived in Stornoway not just Mondays to Fridays but on at least some weekends.[75] So by now the school was indeed serving as a secondary school for the wider island. Maclean was probably too early to have benefitted much, if at all, from the £10 scholarships designed for such rural pupils – see SSB minute of 10 December 1894; but census data show that his father was a village merchant living in a substantial Bragar house.**

HMI Report:[76]

> *An expensive building of the most modern type is being constructed for the accommodation of secondary pupils both of the Burgh and of the Landward parts of the island... I have much gratification in reporting that the general results are most encouraging.* (LNI)

---

74 "a handsome, black-haired, red-cheeked country boy, my chief competitor" p26 RM MacIver 1968 **As a Tale That Is Told** *Chicago.*
75 We know that, we think, from MacIver's autobiography i.e. it makes reference to Stornoway weekend activities involving Maclean.
76 Certainly by Robertson.

1898

APRIL 1

JL Robertson visited the school today. (LNI)

APRIL 22

The new expensive premises, built and furnished at a cost of over £3000, will soon be ready for occupation. (LNI)

It is indeed gratifying to report that some of the senior pupils have now qualified by Leaving Certificates taken at the school last June for direct entrance to the University and that the bursary competition of the Trust for Education in the Highlands and Islands, several candidates prepared in the school took a high place. (LNI)

Two of these students, Donald Maclean and Robert M MacIver, were to go to university later that year, the first to do so by direct entrance from the Nicolson, Maclean with a bursary of £30 per annum for 4 years; MacIver with one of £25 for 3 years[77] **(respectively £3500 and £2900 per annum at 2014 prices). See Chapter 6 for some more comments on MacIver's bursary.**

Several pupils received a Merit Certificate (awarded for high performance to pupils over the age of 13): one was D Mackenzie. (LNI). **This was the Donald Mackenzie of Aird who was to be Nicolson dux in 1900 and subsequently a professor in the 1930s at Princeton Theological Seminary. Unlike Maclean (Dux 1897) and MacIver (Dux 1898), Mackenzie came from no merchant class background. Son of a single mother, his uncles and aunts were mostly crofting and fishing folk. He probably did rely greatly on the £10 bursary.[78] See Chapter 7 for more about him.**

---

77   1897–1898 Nicolson School Report.
78   And we know from the 1897–98 Nicolson School Report that he held such a bursary.

JULY 1

Medal for Gaelic: Donald Maclean
Dux: Robert M MacIver (LNI)

AUGUST 29

The new Secondary School was formally opened today. (LNI)

That was the Francis St building, the only pre-20th
century Nicolson Institute building which survives to
this day, although it has been long abandoned as a school
building.

1900

MARCH 30

School inspected by JL Robertson. (LNI)

MAY 29

HMI Report[79]
> *As to its Secondary Department, the School is in the very first*
> *rank in the County.*

> *Upper department is recognised... as a separate Secondary*
> *Department.*

1900 Dux and Classics medallist: Donald Mackenzie. (LNI)

OCTOBER 19

Donald Mackenzie passes Arts Preliminary Exam for the
University of Aberdeen. (LNI)[80]
If Gibson (and other heads) had played a large part
in this at secondary school level and if Robertson (and
other HMCIs in Scotland) had played a big part at school
district level, another Scot, one Andrew Carnegie, also

---

79 Probably based on the March 30th inspection.
80 Presumably aiming for entrance in 1901.

made a very decisive intervention in 1901. One can think of Carnegie as a 19th century Donald Trump. Although he has a better claim than Trump to Scottish ancestry and (at least in his later years) a more secure record in philanthropy.

In 1901, Andrew Carnegie decided he would give about $5m to Scottish universities (at today's prices possibly about a quarter billion US dollars, although these conversions are tricky). But, never himself having been near a university, he took some advice and decided it should go into a trust which might be expected to generate a spending power of about £50,000 a year to pay tuition fees for poor students. £50,000 per year was about what the state then spent annually on Scottish universities and is over £2.5m a year at today's prices. Scottish university principals (an unchanging breed to this day) were unimpressed: the money would in essence go to students rather than to them. So Carnegie doubled his investment; and gave the annual investment income from the "new" half to universities for capital build – for example much of the still-standing science build in the early 20th century in the University of Glasgow and the magnificent organ in the Bute Hall came from Carnegie.[81]

The Carnegie Trust itself today says:

> *To put this in context, it should be stressed that, contrary to what is suggested, access to university education in Scotland has not always been free. On the contrary, fees were charged by the universities (originally by the professors directly) which represented a significant barrier to access, and there was no provision for subsistence. There was hot competition for the small number of available bursaries, and the award of a bursary*

81   pp 86, 100 N Haynes 2013 **Building Knowledge: An architectural history of the University of Glasgow** *Edinburgh* & *Glasgow*.

was, within living memory, the occasion of a school holiday. It is precisely because student fees constituted such a serious barrier to entry for the 'qualified and deserving' that Carnegie was first persuaded to consider this endowment.[82]

By 1904, half of all Scottish university undergraduates were benefitting from the Carnegie endowment.[83] **An excellent summary of the effect can be found in another Anderson publication.**[84] **It was hard enough for Robertson, Maclean and MacIver, all sons of prosperous families, to make their ways to university in the 19**th **century. But in the early 20**th **century, Carnegie made a further difference in opening up pathways to universities.**

1901

Donald Mackenzie, Ross-shire County Committee bursary £25 for 3 years.[85] **At 2014 prices that is about £2750 per year.**

1902

JULY:

In the school log it is noted that Murdo Morrison from Tong is a teacher at £130 per annum (LNI) **(just over £14000 at 2014 prices; note also that in 2014 the starting salary for a teacher in Scotland was almost £22,000). He subsequently became Director of Education for Inverness-shire and lived to the age of 99.**

82   http://www.gov.scot/Resource/Doc/82254/0115599.pdf.

83   p288 RD Anderson 1983 **Education & Opportunity in Victorian Scotland** *Edinburgh*.

84   p132 RD Anderson et al 2003 **The University of Edinburgh: An illustrated history** *Edinburgh*.

85   p6 1999 **The Nicolson Institute 125th Anniversary Magazine** *Stornoway*.

1903

Lord Balfour of Burleigh and JL Robertson HMI visit the school.[86]

JULY:

The Board addresses the issue of school students being in residence in Stornoway. They determined to provide "*a home for the lads in town where they would be better cared for than was the case at present.*" (SSB) **There is no reference to "lassies" although by then the school had several in the secondary department, albeit perhaps few from rural areas.**

SEPT:

After at most 2 years on the staff of The Nicolson Institute, Murdo Morrison departs to a post of "*sub-inspector of schools*". He goes with the Board's "*highest approbation.*" (SSB)

An "*epidemic of German measles*" is recorded in the log **(a common feature of school logs of the time)**. (LNI)

OCT:

The (school) bursary competition has 8 entries, 4 from Carloway. (SSB)

1904

Mary Crichton (Dux of 1901) returns to the school, initially temporarily, as a teacher. **Locally educated teachers were unusual at that time, at least in the upper parts of the school.**

By November, new build was in progress for infants and juniors and was due to open in 1905. (SSB)

---

86 Alexander Hugh Bruce, 6th Lord Balfour of Burleigh, was Secretary of State for Scotland between 1895 and 1903.

An outbreak of whooping cough is reported. By Nov 21st, it shuts the infant department for some time. (LNI)

1905

It is recorded, as of June 30, that the school has 147 infant students, 430 elementary ones and 146 secondary students. **By then, although this is not recorded in the log, "secondary" students become so by passing a "qualifying exam" about the age of 12; those who fail must remain in school in post-elementary classes to the age of 14.** (LNI)

December

On Dec 7, the clock and chimes for the tower[87] are handed over. A speech by Anderson (Chair, Parish School Board) quotes extensively from a letter from the two surviving Nicolson brothers (Roderick and Kenneth[88]) in which they make reference to over 700 students "some from the Hebrides and from opposite shores of Ross and Inverness-shire". This, while strictly accurate, can lead one to overlook that fact that the vast majority of the 700 was from the town of Stornoway itself.

The title of "Headmaster" is changed to "Rector" **(as it remains to this day)**. (SSB)

1906

748 on the roll. There is a reference to the "Qualifying Exam".

July 14:

The Female Industrial School in Stornoway closes. 85 or so students are thereby added to the roll of The Nicolson Institute.

---

87   See picture on page 77.
88   p3 1973 **The Nicolson Institute Centenary School Magazine** *Stornoway.*

The resulting school congestion is solved by school students from Battery Park going to Sandwickhill School and school students from Coulegrein going to Laxdale School. **Certainly the latter part of that arrangement lasted for many years.**[89] (LNI)

There are 4 four pupil teacher candidates from The Nicolson Institute for the "King's Scholarship Exam" and 43 Lewis candidates in all, 19 of them students from The Nicolson Institute. **The others would have been from rural Lewis schools, which typically had one or two pupil teachers each. Pupil teachers, as we have seen, were school students who did a mixture of teaching and of advanced school study and who were paid – modestly – for that. Every year they could compete for a "King's Scholarship" or, prior to 1901, a "Queen's Scholarship" that took them to a training college for a two-year teacher training course. In 1906, the whole system was in the midst of a radical reform, including the abolition of the role of pupil teacher.**[90]

1907

The school log records the story of Jane A Fraser. A school student in 1889, she had become a pupil teacher in July 1900; in September 1902 she had won a "King's Scholarship, 1st Class" which had taken her to the Church of Scotland Training College in Edinburgh **(now the Moray House School of Education)** for 2 years of study and then a year of study abroad **(then as now needed for those who intended to teach a foreign language)**. So she had returned to The Nicolson Institute as a certificated teacher in 1905. But now she was dead. **She could not have guessed that her brief life would provide, more than 100 years later, a vivid illustration of a scheme of**

89   p46 C Smith 2001 **Around the Peat-Fire** *Edinburgh.*
90   p138 M Cruickshank 1970 **History of the Training of Teachers in Scotland** *Edinburgh.*

teacher training which was then widespread but is now almost forgotten. (LNI)

> *In 1907, with a school roll of more than 800, a decision was made to erect a new building in Springfield to relieve the now overcrowded Secondary Department in Francis Street. This new building was built with the aid of a £7,000 grant from the Scottish Education department and incorporated five classrooms, a science laboratory, technical workshop and art room. The new building was opened in 1910 and adjacent to this, a gymnasium was erected, paid for by money received from the estates of the last surviving brothers of the Founder, Alexander Morrison Nicolson. The total benefactions of the Nicolson family to the School amounted to almost £20,000. In 1931, a new School badge was adopted with a most appropriate design of five lit torches, symbolising the school's founder and his brothers.*[91]

1908

There are 810 in the school, 250 in secondary department, of whom 80 are "living away from home" in "approved lodgings". (LNI)

JULY:

5 gain full Leaving Certificate.
There is a reference to "Pryde's School" **Pryde was the "second master" and i/c elementary classes.**
11 sit the King's Scholarship Exam **(the distinctive gateway to teacher training college)**. (LNI)

1909

JULY:

7 gain full Leaving Certificate.

---

91   http://www.stornowayhistoricalsociety.org.uk/the-nicolson-institute.html.

Murdo Murray is school dux. **Quite a lot, as we shall see, is known and written about Murray, the son of a Back shoemaker. Graduating in 1913 with an MA from Aberdeen, he went initially to teach in Paible HG School. He fought in the Great War and wrote well-known Gaelic war poems.[92] He became an HMI, inspected some Lewis schools and, in retirement, survived until 1964. He was a chronicler of the life of John Munro, dux in 1911.[93] The** school report also records John Munro to be first in Class IV. (LNI)

1910[94]

APRIL 14:

The secondary department has:

23 school students from the parish of Barvas

29 from the parish of Uig;

37 from the parish of Lochs;

6 from Harris; 2 from Barra; and

55 from the "landward" part of the parish of Stornoway i.e. from outside the burgh of Stornoway.

This total of 152 represents a huge advance on the 1897 position where the equivalent total was 10. But the burgh of Stornoway had another 150 in secondary education. Given that Stornoway at the time had perhaps one-fifth of the Lewis population, rural school students were clearly still under-represented.

---

92   One of them recently re-published.

93   Information courtesy of Iain Gordon Macdonald and of Ruairidh Maciver.

94   The primary data from here on are from annual Nicolson Institute school reports or the somewhat intermittent Nicolson Institute school magazines rather than from parish board minutes or the school log.

Maggie Stewart is school dux. **(Something is known about her, not least from an obituary in the 1962 school magazine. For she spent the bulk of her adult career as a teacher in the Nicolson Institute.)** Jane Gibson (Rector's daughter) has the elementary school prize. **She was dux in 1916 and spent her career in teaching in the Edinburgh area. It was she about 1963 who retrieved what was thought to be a long-lost poem by John Munro and sent it to Murdo Murray, who in turn sent it to The Nicolson Institute.**[95]

£6400 **(about £670,000 at 2014 prices)** is being invested in constructing the "Pentland Building" **i.e. the only 20ᵗʰ century school building which remains in use by The Nicolson Institute to this day.**

1911

John Munro is school dux and is also awarded the maths and science prizes. **Graduating in 1914 with an MA from Aberdeen, he fought in the Great War, wrote well-known Gaelic war poems and was killed in 1918.**[96]

There are references to the "Secondary Education Committee" in Dingwall. **While state-financed schools were the responsibility of parish school boards from 1872 to 1918, much of the special finance allocated for developing "higher grade" i.e. secondary departments was, as we have already noted, overseen at County Council level from 1892 onwards. In the Dingwall-based Ross and Cromarty County, which covered Lewis, JL Robertson HMCI was a pivotal figure.**

---

95   As we shall see in Chapter 8.
96   See http://lewis-lost-ww1.blogspot.co.uk/2012/03/john-munro-27-aignish.html
His wider story is told in Chapter 8.

1913

An outbreak of German measles closes the school for 3 weeks.

1914

The school magazine reports that of school students of
The Nicolson Institute of the last 16 years i.e. since 1898, 65
had graduated from the University of Aberdeen, 11 from the
University of Edinburgh and 23 from the University of Glasgow.

1917

There is a report of discussions to build two school hostels in
Stornoway for school students from rural areas, one for boys, one
for girls. **And indeed by then the Carnegie UK Trust had a
specialist "hostels" committee in place.**

1922

JULY 14.

> *Miss Haldane stated that the Hostel at Stornoway... would be
> ready for occupation on 12ᵗʰ or 14ᵗʰ August, and the Secretary had
> been instructed to employ Messrs Ross and Connell to transfer the
> building, etc., to the Education Authority. Miss Haldane had been
> asked by the Authority to allow her name to be associated with
> the Hostel, but had pointed out that this was out of the question,
> since it must be connected officially with the Trust. There was
> a certain difficulty in calling it simply the "Carnegie Hostel,"
> since this might, for some time at least, suggest that it was called
> after the previous owners of the building. After discussion it was
> decided that the name be the 'Louise Carnegie Hostel' in honour
> of Mrs Carnegie, subject, of course, to her approval.*[97]

---

97   Carnegie United Kingdom Trust Archives.

The Louise Carnegie hostel – for female secondary school
students of The Nicolson Institute from rural areas – opens.[98]
**It was on the site now occupied by An Lanntair, the
cultural centre of modern Stornoway. The hostel was not
a new building, having previously been the Imperial Hotel.**

1928

The list of secondary school students includes a John Smith
from 23 New Valley.[99]

MAY 11

> *Miss Haldane, the Secretary, and the Architect visited Stornoway
> on 7th–8th April. Excellent progress had been made with the Boys'
> Hostel, and there was every expectation that it would be ready
> for occupation at the commencement of the term in August. Miss
> Haldane reported that she was very pleased with the appearance
> of the Hostel. She had given instructions regarding decoration and
> linoleum, and had accepted a tender for the supply of domestic
> equipment. Other estimates would be ready for the July Meeting.
> Meanwhile, the Committee agreed to the provision of a flag-
> staff, a piano, a set of indoor games, a library, and the adaptation
> of the garden for the playing of Badminton. It was decided to
> ask the Authority to fix the Opening Ceremony for a date when
> the boys would be in residence, and to invite Mrs Carnegie to
> be present. Miss Haldane would represent the Trustees, and
> the Chairman would be present if possible. The Committee
> approved the suggestion that the name of the Hostel should be
> 'The Elizabeth Haldane Hostel' and decided to recommend this
> to the Authority.[100]*

---

98   http://www.carnegieuktrust100.org.uk/timeline/.
99   He appears in the next chapter.
100   Carnegie United Kingdom Trust Archives.

1929

The Nicolson Institute school magazine celebrates the achievements of, among others, RM MacIver (Dux, 1898) and Donald Mackenzie (Dux, 1900).

It carries a story of the opening of the Louise Carnegie Hostel in 1922 and of the Elizabeth Haldane Hostel[101] (for boys) in 1928, the latter named after Elizabeth Haldane of Cloan. **She was the first female member (1914) of Andrew Carnegie's United Kingdom Trust.[102] The financing of the two hostels came from the UK Carnegie Trust, as we have seen, as did finance for a school hostel in Portree. Her late brother, as we shall see in Chapter 11, had made a speech in the House of Lords in 1916 extolling the virtues of The Nicolson Institute. Given that they came from Auchterarder and that they both spent much of their careers in London, it is not entirely clear why they evinced such a fondness for education in Lewis.**

1930

The school magazine ("3rd post-War edition") includes:

• A contribution by Agnes Mure Mackenzie, **a Stornoway-born student of The Nicolson Institute in the 1910s who subsequently achieved fame as a writer.**

• A reference to an ex-school student who is now in Edinburgh University, one Hector MacIver.[103]

• A note that Murdo Murray (Dux 1909) had migrated from a school in Beauly to become His Majesty's Inspector of Schools.

---

101 https://en.wikipedia.org/wiki/Elizabeth_Haldane.
102 http://iainthepict.blogspot.co.uk/2011/05/elizabeth-sanderson-haldane.html.
103 He appears in Chapter 10.

5

AN ORDINARY SHAWBOST FAMILY

BY

IAIN SMITH[104], ANN MENNIE[105]
& JOAN FORREST

———

For Iain and Ann, our grandfather Murdo was
one of eight siblings born between 1873 and 1891.
Murdo and our grandmother Annabella then had
nine children born between 1908 and 1928. One was
Iain's father; another was Ann's mother. The lives of
the eight of our grandparents' generation differed
somewhat from the nine of our parents' generation.
The differences, we believe, are systemic; and
typical of the respective times.

---

104   Eldest grandson of Murdo and Annabella.
105   Eldest granddaughter of Murdo and Annabella.

I. Murdo and Annabella

Murdo Smith was born in North Bragar on 22nd June 1883. He was the son of Mary (née Campbell) and of John, married 1872.[106] Murdo had three older brothers: **Norman** (born 1873),[107] **Finlay** (born 1878)[108] and **John** (born 1881).[109] He then acquired two younger brothers: **Donald** (born 1885)[110] and **Kenneth** (born 1891).[111] Murdo also had two sisters: **Effie** (born 1876) and **Catherine** (born 1888).[112, 113]

Summary Table

Parents	John and Mary
Children	Norman b 1873
	Effie b 1876
	Finlay b 1878
	John b 1881
	Murdo b 1883
	Donald b 1885
	Catherine b 1888
	Kenneth b 1891

---

106 From Murdo's birth certificate, viewed 15/4/2014; and 1891 census data; see also p257 J Macleod 2009 **When I Heard the Bell** *Edinburgh*; and also from a family tree from our cousin Jonathan Smith.

107 Birth certificate viewed 9/5/2014; and 1891 census data.

108 Birth certificate viewed 10/5/2014; and 1891 census data.

109 Birth certificate viewed 10/5/2014; and 1891 census data.

110 Birth certificate viewed 10/5/2014 and 1891 census data.

111 Birth certificate viewed 10/5/2014 and 1901 census data.

112 1901 census data; and birth certificate viewed 7/2014.

113 Birth certificate viewed 10/5/2014; 1891 census data.

In the 1881 census (3 April 1881) there was a 5-yr-old daughter "Eric";
*the 1901 census showed up a 25-yr-old **Effie** resident at 14 North Bragar*
*with **Norman, Murdo, Donald, Kenneth** and **Catherine**. We had*
however initially failed to trace her birth certificate. We now looked in
the parish of Barvas for girls called "Eric" born about 1875; and they
*abound. **Effie** (recorded, even on her birth certificate, as "Eric") was born*
on 5th January 1876; and was the daughter of i) John Smith "fisherman",
and apparently illiterate, judging by his cross on the certificate: hence in
no position to correct the Registrar's – recurring – error with "Effie"'s;
and ii) Mary née Campbell. The "Eric" appears to be a mistaken
transliteration of a Gaelic variant of "Effie". This probably explains
why the island to this day has "Erica" as a reasonably common name for
native-born girls; and a distinct shortage of native-born "Eric"'s.

*So **Murdo** did indeed have an older sister **Effie** as well as a*
*younger sister **Catherine**.*

SCHOOLING

All the siblings, boys and girls, seem to have attended school
from age 5 to about age 13 in consistency with the laws – although
not always the practice – of the times. **Murdo** – and his siblings
– became literate, albeit not in their native language. We certainly
know that **Murdo** became an avid reader of books and of
political journals.[114]

CROFTS

Murdo, although he engaged in crofting in Bragar from an
early age, had at no time any crofting tenure or rights either to
house or to land. These rights, enshrined in the Crofters Holdings
(Scotland) Act 1886, were generally destined for the first-born.
This is a system common in much of Europe for at least 1000
years, one which lives on and it has led to much sea-borne
migration, some temporary and some permanent, by younger
landless brothers. The legendary Vikings were only the best
known examples: **Murdo, John, Donald**, and **Kenneth** were

---

114   p139 C Smith 2001 **Around the Peat-Fire** *Edinburgh.*

to follow, some departing further and more permanently than others. Professor Devine is generally informative on this issue.[115] Although, for working class rural Hebrideans, the issue only achieved real relevance in the late 19th century and onwards.

Much of the family history that follows is by **Murdo**'s second son *Calum*.[116] His daughter Marjory helped to shape his manuscript into publishable form.

MURDO SPREADS HIS WINGS

Murdo joined the Royal Naval Reserve (a maritime equivalent of the better-known Territorial Army) in 1899, giving his age as 18 rather than 16.[117] Many of his male contemporaries, including three of his brothers, did the same. RNR records[118] show a Murdo Smith of North Bragar giving his date of birth as 12 May 1881. We have also found RNR records for his three brothers. The match of the dates of birth on them with birth certificate data is erratic. For all who joined, including **Murdo**, there were beneficial and welcome financial consequences i.e. an annual payment. For some of them, but not for **Murdo**, there were other consequences which were deadly.

About the same time, **Murdo** went fishing for several months each year, following the seasonal herring hunt along the west coast of Scotland; up to Wick, Thurso and Kirkwall; and down the east coast as far as Great Yarmouth and Lowestoft. Along with the itinerant fishermen, who crewed the boats and caught the fish, went the fishing girls, gutting, salting and barrelling the herring; and transported, mostly by sea, sometimes by train and (once only, and memorably) by plane,[119] around the various fishing ports.

This was a migratory industry which went on until the 1950s; but had peaked from about 1850 or so into the 1880s

---

115 pp 4–10 TM Devine 2011 **To The Ends of the Earth** *London*.

116 C Smith 2001 **Around the Peat-Fire** *Edinburgh*.

117 p14 C Smith 2001 **Around the Peat-Fire** *Edinburgh*.

118 http://www.nationalarchives.gov.uk/records/royal-naval-reserve-service-records.htm l/; accessed 7/9/2014.

119 See plaque in Wick airport.

and then again about 1890 to 1913. It looks as if John Smith and his eldest four sons (**Norman**, **Finlay**, **John** and **Murdo** himself) were predominantly fishermen (and RNR reservists) rather than agrarian labourers, at least in their younger years; possibly following the west and east coast migration of herring pre-marriage, and settling for local fishing, probably mostly white fish pursued in sailing boats, post-marriage. Relative to what happened post-1920, the years to 1913 were mostly good for that.[120]

The temporarily migrant Hebridean males and females managed some socialisation, sometimes flamboyant, with each other; and **Murdo** Smith, perhaps 20 years old, met one fisher girl **Annabella** Macleod, daughter of Angus Macleod and of Marion (née Macaulay) from the adjoining village of Shawbost in Lewis. Their partnership was to last more than 50 years.

In Fraserburgh, far from home, on 29th August 1907, **Murdo** and **Annabella** married;[121] and the newly married couple, on returning home, lived on a croft at 48 North Shawbost with Murdo's father-in-law and mother-in-law. The father-in-law tenanted the croft: he had no sons, but two daughters, one of them **Annabella**. The elder daughter Mary Macleod (by then Macaulay) already lived elsewhere in Shawbost with her husband. So neither **Murdo** nor his wife (although they both engaged in crofting) had title to the house or to the land in Shawbost. **Murdo**, at least judging by pre-1920 birth certificates, went on fishing.

---

120 A good summary is at pp20–25 S Matheson 2008 **Reflections on the History of Stornoway and Lewis** *Isle of Lewis.*

121 Marriage certificate viewed 15/4/2014.

Figure 1 John L Robertson (1854–1927): Chapter 1

Figure 2 Dewar Committee: Chapter 1

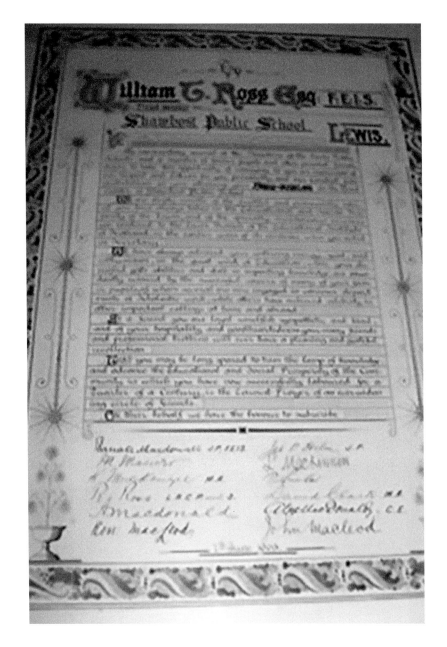

Figure 3 Illuminated address to WT Ross: Chapter 2

Figure 4 Alexander Macdonald 1879–1941: Chapter 3

Figure 5 Bunessan Bay: Chapter 3

Figure 6 Bunessan Church of Scotland: Chapter 3

Figure 7 Bunessan Church of Scotland Manse of the 1930s: Chapter 3

Figure 8 The modern Nicolson Institute of the 21st century, with preserved Clock Tower, circa 1904, from the old school: Chapter 4.

Figure 9 Hyndland School early 20th century building: Chapter 4

Figure 10 Andrew Carnegie: Chapter 4

A first son was born on 20th November 1908.[122] He was called *John*, presumably after his late paternal grandfather. He was Iain Smith's father and Ann Mennie's maternal uncle.

Murdo's second son, or the second to survive infancy, *Calum*[123] was born on 29th May 1912. Two preceding boys, also called Calum, had not survived for more than 3 weeks of infancy.[124]

A daughter was born on 5th January 1914 and named *Mary Ann*.[125] She was Ann Mennie's mother and Iain Smith's paternal aunt.

In 1914 **Murdo** went to war in the navy i.e. mobilised with his older brothers **Norman**, **Finlay** and **John**;[126] and remained away from home for much of the time until May 1919. In Bragar, approximately 145 people did war service. Of these, 92 had pre-War been in the RNR (almost all of them would have been fishermen) and were mobilised on 4 August 1914 – by Winston Churchill – to serve in the Royal Navy. 12 of these died during the War, and then 7 drowned on 1 January 1919 on the *Iolaire*.

In Shawbost, **Annabella** and her parents tilled the land, cut peats, spun wool and weaved tweed: the years 1903 to 1906 had seen considerable growth in the Harris Tweed industry, although it was the 1930s before it became highly significant.[127]

In late 1916 Angus Macleod died (ie **Murdo**'s father-in-law and **Annabella**'s father).[128] The title of the house and tenancy rights of the croft passed to sister-in-law Mary Macaulay. But, given that both her husband and **Murdo** were mostly away at war, this had no immediate effect. Shortly afterwards a third

---

122   Birth certificate viewed 15/4/2014.
123   Birth certificate viewed 17/4/2014.
124   C Smith 2001 **Around the Peat-Fire** *Edinburgh.*
125   Birth certificate viewed 06/5/2014.
126   p191, Grant W 1920: digitised 2013 **"Loyal Lewis": Roll of Honour** at https://archive.org/stream/loyallewisrollof1920 National Library of Scotland.
127   http://www.harristweed.org/about-us/ accessed 8/9/2014.
128   p15 C Smith 2001 **Around the Peat-Fire** *Edinburgh.*

son was born to **Murdo** and **Annabella** on 27th April 1917[129] and – unsurprisingly – called *Angus*.

Murdo's brother **John** aged 37 of 11 South Shawbost, with 180 fellow-islanders and some 20 ship's crew, drowned in the *Iolaire* disaster on his return journey to Lewis on 1 January 1919.[130] **John** left a widow and four children.[131] He is buried in Bragar.

In a documented and heartbreaking story, his widow was faced with a formidable questionnaire to confirm her entitlement to six months of financial support[132]

> *At 11 North* [sic][133]*Shawbost on 11 February 1919, Mrs Kate Smith stared at this cold bit of paper with all its boxes and dotted lines. She was thirty-six, her life given over to that of a wife – well, it had been – and mother of four little children: Catherine, nine; and John, seven; and Maggie, five; and Maryann, a mite of two-and-a-half. John Smith deckhand had served on HMS Duchess of Devonshire. He had been thirty-five* [sic]*. He had just been buried at Bragar. She would continue to receive £2 16s 4d [£2.81, or approx. £100 at today's prices] of a weekly allowance- until 30 June 1919. The question was blunt: 'Relationship to Sailor?'*
>
> *Mrs Smith thought, and wrote 'He was my Beloved Husband'.*

Murdo returned safely in mid-1919 and resumed crofting (and carting).

In 1920, a second daughter was born on 17th June,[134] to be called *Johanna* after her recently deceased uncle **John**. (A contemporaneous first cousin of *Johanna's*, the daughter

---

129 Birth certificate viewed 07/5/2014.

130 p257 J Macleod 2009 **When I Heard the Bell** *Edinburgh*.

131 p199, Grant W 1920: digitised 2013 **"Loyal Lewis": Roll of Honour** at https://archive.org/stream/loyallewisrollof1920 National Library of Scotland.

132 p187-8 J Macleod 2009 **When I Heard the Bell** *Edinburgh*.

133 Actually 11 South Shawbost. See 2014 **Eachdraidh Nan Croitean** Dalbeg and Shawbost.

134 Birth certificate viewed 07/5/2014.

of **Finlay**, was dubbed Johnina. Life, even at christening, added unwanted handicaps to Hebrideans of the female gender.)

The tenancy of the croft at 48 North Shawbost was reclaimed without acrimony by **Murdo**'s sister-in-law Mary (to whom it belonged) and her husband John Macaulay.

MIGRATION FROM VILLAGE TO TOWN.

At some point between July 1920 and August 1923, **Murdo, Annabella** and family migrated – to near the town of Stornoway. Why? Broadly there were four possible reasons:

1. A general post-War economic depression; although some 720,000 UK service personnel had died between 1914 and 1919 and some 800,000 had been maimed, some 2 million able-bodied males, including **Murdo**, had been demobilised and returned to an unforgiving and unpromising labour market.[135]

2. The loss of access to crofting land; and crop failure in 1922/1923, well recorded by Hutchison and by Hunter.[136]

3. The prospect of urban employment.

4. Decline of fishing. The herring, cod and ling were still there: the days of unsustainable over-fishing and species extinction awaited the replacement of drift nets with trawl nets and of serendipitous searching for fish shoals with sonar and other technological wonders.[137] But other factors intervened: a declining fish market was increasingly dominated by steam trawlers.[138] In all the birth certificates up to 1920, **Murdo** is described as "fisherman". In all the

---

135 Chapters 10 & 14 N Ferguson 1998 **The Pity of War 1914–1918** *London.*
136 p217 R Hutchinson 2003 **The Soap Man: Lewis, Harris and Lord Leverhulme** *Edinburgh*; p341 J Hunter 1999 **Last of the Free: A History of the Highlands and Islands of Scotland** *Edinburgh.*
137 pp 593–595 L Paine 2013 **The Sea and Civilization: A maritime history of the world** *London.*
138 p268 J Hunter 2000 **The Making of the Crofting Community** New Edition *Edinburgh.*

birth certificates after 1923, **Murdo** is described as "general labourer". We return to this later.

*Murdo's brother **Kenneth** also land-dispossessed had taken earlier and even more radical migratory action back in 1911. We have traced his emigration record: he had sailed from Glasgow to Montreal, ominously on the Cassandra, departing 22nd April 1911 for a job as a labourer. He was killed in Canada on a construction site in 1922.*

In 1923, twins were born on 1st August at 16 Laxdale: *Annabella* and *Kenneth Murdo*, the latter called after his recently deceased paternal uncle and after his father. *John*, their 14-yr-old eldest brother, registered their births.[139] So now there were 7 children.

Between 1924 and 1933, they lived in the village of New Valley, about one mile outside the town of Stornoway.

*In 1926, a third one of **Murdo's** brothers, **Donald**, died in Stornoway of tuberculosis aged 41, having followed a merchant navy sea-faring career.[140] **Murdo's** mother Mary, still alive in Bragar at the age of 76 or so,[141] had now seen the death of three of her sons: she herself was to die in 1932.*

Murdo and **Annabella** had an eighth child on 8 May 1926 at 23 New Valley:[142] they called him *Donald John* after two of his deceased paternal uncles.

The last child *Donald Murdo* was born on 3rd May 1928.[143] He was called after his maternal great grandfather and his maternal great great grandfather.[144] *Calum's* book explains that the multiple and combinatorial use of the names John, Murdo, and Donald was not an issue for **Murdo** and **Annabella**: each use referred to a separate ancestor.

---

139   Birth certificate viewed 07/5/2014.
140   Death certificate viewed 11/5/2014.
141   The census records and the death certificate are not well-aligned.
142   Birth certificate viewed 07/5/2014.
143   Birth certificate viewed 07/5/2014.
144   p116 C Smith 2001 **Around the Peat-Fire** *Edinburgh*.

Parents	**Murdo and Annabella**
Children	John b 1908
	Malcolm/Calum b 1912
	Mary Ann b 1914
	Angus b 1917
	Johanna b 1920
	Annabella b 1923
	Kenneth Murdo b 1923
	Donald John b 1926
	Donald Murdo b 1928

In 1933, the family moved from the private tenancy in New Valley into a much superior municipally owned house in Stornoway itself.[145]

*Finlay, **Murdo**'s brother and senior to him by five years, died aged 62 at 14 North Bragar on 25th June 1941.[146] **Murdo**'s eldest brother **Norman** died at 11 North Bragar aged 70 in December 1944.[147] So now all his five brothers were dead.*

Murdo worked, still a labourer, until his retirement in 1948. He had been almost forced to retire in 1946, the false age he had given to the RNR in 1899 (see above) having been carried forward into other government records.[148] He was left with almost 10 years: to read, to preside over weekly political debates with sons and daughters still in Lewis and to teach draughts to the eldest of his grandchildren.

Murdo and **Annabella** celebrated their golden wedding in 1957, with 8 of their 9 children and with the bridesmaid of 1907 present.

Murdo died in 1958; and **Annabella**, having lived her latter years with her daughter *Annabella*, in 1966.

---

145 p128 C Smith 2001 **Around the Peat-Fire** *Edinburgh*.
146 Death certificate viewed 11/5/2014.
147 Death certificate viewed 11/5/2014.
148 p14 C Smith 2001 **Around the Peat-Fire** *Edinburgh*.

2. COMPARING GENERATIONS

To recapitulate, they were the children of John Smith (1845–1894) and of Mary Campbell (of Arnol descent; died 1932).

Norman (1873–1944). *Fisherman; RN sailor; and crofter.*

Effie (1876–?).

Finlay (1878–1941). *Fisherman; RN sailor; and crofter.*[149]

John (1881–1919). *Fisherman; RN sailor.*

Murdo (1883–1958). *Fisherman; RN sailor; crofter; road labourer.*

Donald (1885–1926). *Merchant navy sailor.*

Catherine (1888–?).

Kenneth (1891–1922). *Construction site worker in Canada.*

NOTABLE SUMMARY POINTS:

1.   All were educated to the age of 13; but none subsequently stayed on in education.

2.   All the males worked in manual occupations, occupations which had existed for centuries. Mostly they worked with old technologies: wooden boats, sails, oars, long lines, drift nets, horse-driven ploughs and carts, spades, picks and shovels.

3.   Only two of the six brothers lived to the age of 65 and none of them beyond the age of 75.

---

149   Four of Finlay's grand-daughters achieved musical fame in the 1960s as the Macdonald Sisters. The oldest one Kathleen is a graduate of what is now the Royal Conservatoire of Scotland.

Murdo (1883–1958) and his wife **Annabella** (1883–1966), as we have seen, had 9 children who grew up to adulthood:

i) *John* (1908–1970) School Headteacher

ii) *Calum/Malcolm*[150] (1912–2003) Scottish Hydro-Electric Board office worker

iii) *Mary Ann* (1914–1984) GPO career

iv) *Angus* (1917–1994) Motor mechanic

v) *Johanna* (1920–1977) Housekeeper

vi) *Annabella* (1923–2005) Telephone Exchange operator, then supervisor

vii) *Kenneth Murdo* (1923–1992) Oil tanker driver

viii) *Donald John* (1926–2014) Artist and art teacher

ix) *Donald Murdo* (1928–2007) Factor, Stornoway Trust

NOTABLE SUMMARY POINTS:

1.   All were educated at least to the age of 14; three – all males – went on to higher education, a high proportion for children of the early 20th century.[151]

2.   Six worked in non-manual occupations.

3.   Four worked in occupations which were technology-driven creations of the late 19th/early 20th centuries. All of them at work, and at home, used what were then modern technologies: notably telephones and cars.

4.   Seven of the nine lived to the age of 65 or beyond; and five of them beyond the age of 75.

---

150   Christened by the former (Gaelic) name; birth registered under the latter (English) version.

151   p406 TM Devine 2012 **The Scottish Nation: A Modern History** *London.*

1.   Generation B lived longer than Generation A.

2.   Generation B had some access to higher education; Generation A had none. School and university bursaries of the early 20th century played a role in that; as did **Murdo's** unusually positive views on such matters.

3.   Generation B worked predominantly in non-manual middle-class occupations; Generation A exclusively in manual working-class occupations.

4.   Technological innovations of the late 19th century and of the 20th century (motor-cars; electrical power; telephones) influenced the occupations of some of generation B. And came to influence the domestic lives of all of them – but only the latter years of the longer-lived of generation A.

5.   Changes in the fishing industry influenced the lives of the Generation A, sometimes for good, latterly for ill. They had little impact on Generation B.

As Hunter makes clear, trends in 19th century agriculture, of which more below, made the population of Lewis, which grew from 20,000 to 30,000 in the later 19th century, more dependent on other forms of income, notably on fishing.[152] Hunter estimates that in the 1860s and 70s as many as 5000 Lewis male crofters, perhaps well over half of all rural adult males in Lewis, went for two months annually to Wick to work at the herring fishing.[153] The 1880s, when **Murdo** was born in Bragar, were initially not good in that respect.[154] A seasonal wage of perhaps £20 or £30 in 1883 (£3000 at 2014

---

152   p180 J Hunter 2000 **The Making of the Crofting Community** New Edition *Edinburgh.*

153   p292 J Hunter 1999 **Last of the Free: A History of the Highlands and Islands of Scotland** *Edinburgh.*

154   p237 J Hunter 2000 **The Making of the Crofting Community** New Edition *Edinburgh.*

prices) had declined to £1 or £2 by 1887: an abundance of herring had saturated the market. But, in 1888, both the white fish and the herring industry experienced an upturn which was to last for some 20 years or more.

By 1891, **Murdo**'s oldest (18-yr-old) brother Norman appears to have been away at the herring season; and brothers Finlay, John and **Murdo** himself were to follow. Almost certainly it was fishing (and the useful Royal Naval Reserve retainer: itself fishing-triggered)[155] which provided most of their cash income up until 1914. Crofting provided a back-up income, largely but not wholly in kind rather than in cash: potatoes, sheep, cattle, oats and peats.

Post 1918, the returning warriors faced a decline of fishing:

i)   the herring were still there, although now the mechanised steam-driven boats – largely from east coast Scotland and east coast England ports – required less crew.

ii)   the 1917 Russian Revolution had closed a major pre-War fishing market i.e. the UK government had decided to close it.

iii)   the local herring boats in west coast Scotland, still largely sail-driven, needed capital investment to replace them, capital which was lacking;[156] and

iv)   the local white fish industry was also in trouble: the local sailboats were no match for the steam-driven boats from the East of Scotland and from elsewhere.[157]

Lord Leverhulme's 1920s plans for a vast white fish industry, firstly in Lewis then in Harris, proved to be illusory.[158]

155   p121 D Macdonald D 1978 **Lewis: A History of the Island** *Edinburgh.*
156   p268 J Hunter 2000 **The Making of the Crofting Community** New Edition *Edinburgh.*
157   See pp 12–13 **Back in the Day** August 2014.
158   R Hutchinson 2003 **The Soap Man: Lewis, Harris and Lord Leverhulme** *Edinburgh*; p341 J Hunter 1999 **Last of the Free: A History of the Highlands and Islands of Scotland** 1999 *Edinburgh.*

This was probably the major factor in **Murdo**'s migration to Stornoway possibly in 1923. (In 1923/24 fifty-six persons emigrated from Bragar and Shawbost to Canada.[159] Most were single males, although not all. **Murdo**'s age and the size of his family would have precluded that option.)

6.   Crofting legislation affected generation A: it affected only the early lives of generation B.

The early years of the 19th century had seen crofts and common pastureland confiscated on an extensive scale across the Highlands and Islands.[160] **Annabella**'s family, on her mother's side, had been cleared from fertile parts of Uig (Reef and Valtos) to the bleakness of Shawbost: in the 1950's **Annabella** could recollect one of her grandmothers, as an old woman circa 1888, still lamenting her own forcible departure – as a child in the early decades of the 19th century – from the abundance of the Uig machair lands.[161]

The Crofters Holdings (Scotland) Act 1886 gave to **Murdo**'s father John, to **Annabella**'s father Angus and to thousands of others: security of tenure; rights to a fair rent; title to the "improvements" on the croft ie the house; and a right to bequeath the croft and croft house. Rents came down by around 20%–30%; and some 72% of the rent arrears in Lewis and Wester Ross – mostly arising from the bad days of the early 1880s – were written off.[162] So Norman and Finlay benefitted from this in Bragar and spent all of their lives there. What the 1886 Act did not give was any rights of extra

159   http://www.abdn.ac.uk/emigration/ **Scottish Emigration Database** University of Aberdeen accessed 26–27th Aug 2014.
160   R Hutchinson 2003 **The Soap Man: Lewis, Harris and Lord Leverhulme** *Edinburgh*; p341 J Hunter 1999 **Last of the Free: A History of the Highlands and Islands of Scotland** 1999 *Edinburgh.*
161   A plausible connection with Uig is seen in one version of our family tree.
162   pp 230-232 TM Devine 1994 **Clanship to Crofters' War** *Manchester*; p320 Hunter J 1999 **Last of the Free: A History of the Highlands and Islands of Scotland** 1999 *Edinburgh.*

land to the landless or the cottar or the squatter. So the other four brothers did not benefit, especially when the Act explicitly forbad sub-letting of crofts.

In Shawbost Angus Macleod (and then in 1919) his older daughter benefitted; but not his younger daughter **Annabella** or her husband **Murdo**.

Elsewhere in Lewis (e.g. in Park, in Aignish and in Melbost) or in Harris (e.g. Taransay) or in the Southern Isles (e.g. Vatersay), the landless aspired to reclaiming nearby land from which their ancestors had been evicted some 50 or more years earlier[163] and ultimately had some if limited success; but the landless in Bragar (and Shawbost and Arnol) had, with the minor exception of Dalbeg and Dalmore, no nearby lands to which to aspire.

So Norman, who inherited his father's croft at 14 North Bragar in 1894, and Finlay remained in Bragar; **Murdo** and John (from 1907 and 1909 respectively) established squatter or cottar possession in Shawbost; and Donald and Kenneth about the same time migrated respectively to careers in the UK merchant marine and in Canada: which is presumably why 1914–19 local war records exist for the first four; but not for the last two.

7. Four sons of Generation A were in the Royal Naval Reserve.[164] As a result they were mobilised on the outbreak of war in 1914. Some writers have described this as "conscription": but conscription did not appear until later in the war.[165] Of these four, three returned safely; John did not.

Of the six males in Generation B, four were conscripted in WWII. All four survived.

163   Chapters 9 & 10 J Hunter 2000 **The Making of the Crofting Community** New Edition *Edinburgh.*
164   p14 C Smith 2001 **Around the Peat-Fire** *Edinburgh.*
165   See, for example, Chapter XXIV R Jenkins 1986 **Asquith** *London* and Chapter 27 R Hattersley 2010 **The Great Outsider: David Lloyd George** *London.*

8.   Of Generation A only **Murdo** lived in municipal housing; and then only 1933–1958, much less than half of his adult life. In urban Scotland of the late 19th century, private rented accommodation was the working class norm; in rural Scotland it was the "tied house" or, in some counties, the "croft house".

7 of the 9 of Generation B spent most of their adult working lives in either rented or "tied" public-sector houses, mostly council housing. *Donald John* (owner-occupier 1958–2014) and *Calum* (owner-occupier 1959–2002) are the exceptions to that.

If one reflects on who owned what houses in Scotland over the last 150 years that makes sense. Glasgow built its first council house scheme only in 1919; and "owner-occupation" was then, and remained for decades, comparatively rare.

9.   The Lewis-based males of Generation A (apart from **Murdo** himself) did not experience: running domestic water; electricity; mains gas. This was partly a function of age, partly of early mortality and partly of rural location.

From 1933 onwards, all of Generation B lived in a house with running water and mains gas and, subsequently, electricity (the house and the mains gas were Lord Leverhulme legacies to a local community trust);[166] and only *John* subsequently ever experienced anything different – for a period in rural Lewis: "the schoolhouse with a bathroom and running water through the taps was looked upon as a little mansion house in the centre of Lionel village."[167] Mansion indeed, but it had no mains gas; the water had to be hand-pumped into the house; and electricity arrived only about 1951, courtesy of the newly created North of Scotland Hydro Electric Board.[168]

---

166   R Hutchinson 2003 **The Soap Man: Lewis, Harris and Lord Leverhulme** *Edinburgh*.

167   Stornoway Gazette 24/7/2014.

168   p558 TM Devine 2012 **The Scottish Nation : A Modern History** *London*; p345 J Hunter 1999 **Last of the Free: A History of the Highlands and Islands of Scotland** *Edinburgh*.

The differences between Generation A and generation B were not wholly random. Many of them can be ascribed to economic, educational, social, military, epidemiological and technological factors.

6

PROFESSOR ROBERT M MACIVER, THE SOCIOLOGIST FROM STORNOWAY

———

Robert Morrison MacIver was born in the town of Stornoway in 1882 and lived as a child first on North Beach Street and then on Bayhead – where, many years later, MacIver's Garage was established by his father. His mother came from a Stornoway family; his father, although living in Stornoway and flourishing as a merchant in the Harris Tweed industry, had come from the village of North Shawbost.

R. M. MacIver died 88 years later in the United States, having established a reputation in the 1920s or so as one of the world's greatest sociologists.

There is no Hebridean who can match the academic accomplishments of Robert M MacIver. MacIver's autobiography *As a Tale That Is Told* (1968) is informative.

MacIver was initially not totally inspired by the Nicolson Institute where he says there were "routine lessons by uninspiring teachers".[169] But, as we have seen (in Chapters 1 and 4) a new headteacher changed the picture.

We can put this in a historical context:

> *In January 1893, the then headmaster, Mr Forbes, was placed in charge of the new Secondary department which introduced the teaching of Latin, Greek, Mathematics, Geography, History, English, French, German, Music, Domestic Economy, Drawing and Needlework. The school was now the most advanced educational centre in the islands and, under the influence of its next headmaster, Mr WJ Gibson in 1894, the Nicolson really began to take off. Gibson was one of the greatest and most enlightened educationalists of his day and in his later years, was awarded the CBE for his efforts – the first headmaster in Scotland to be so honoured.*

> *Mention should be made of the growing importance of the Secondary Department. In 1898 the first two pupils to leave the Nicolson and enter directly into University were Donald Maclean of Bragar to Aberdeen and Robert M MacIver of Stornoway to Edinburgh, each of whom graduated with first class honours and went on to have distinguished academic careers. From then, and up to the present day, there have been an ever increasing number of pupils proceeding from the Nicolson into tertiary education.[170]*

MacIver's testimony to the effect of a new head some 120 years ago is worth quoting today. For it would stand up rather well to what is written currently about how schools achieve excellence:

169   p16 RM MacIver 1968 **As a Tale That Is Told** *Chicago*
170   http://www.stornowayhistoricalsociety.org.uk/index.php?option=com_content&view=article&id=93:nicolsoninstitute&catid=36:features&Itemid=74 Accessed 27/12/11

*The changeover was a turning point in my life. There was now
something to strive for. Paths were opening to the future. When
I heard there were to be prizes for excellence, I felt it was a
call to me, and I was eager to respond. The new discipline was
an uncomfortable shock to our school habits. Our listlessness
met with sharp reprimands. Punctuality was insisted upon.
Homework, negligible before, was imposed, although not
excessively. But once the initiation stage was over schooling
became meaningful to most of us. Something had been missing
from my life, and now I knew what it was. I owe a great debt to
this headteacher – W.J. Gibson – and in retrospect I realise that
I never properly acknowledged it. In youth we take so many gifts
as if they had dropped from the sky.[171]*

And his distinction between the "traditional routinised
fashion" in which his maths teacher taught and the absence of
an "inkling of the beauty of mathematical reasoning or of its
significance for some understanding of the spatial framework of
all that exists" would also stand up well to modern distinctions
between surface rote learning and deep meaningful learning.[172]

In his leisure time, MacIver enjoyed aspects of Stornoway now
gone – some long ago, and some more recently:

*I visited the lofts where they repaired the sails, the boat-building
yards, the spaces under the docks where they worked on the piles,
the smoky pungent-smelling line of sheds where the herring was
kippered.[173]*

MacIver, aged 16, approached the question of going to
university. This would have been, as we have seen above, in
1898, exactly three years before Carnegie scholarships preceded
(long preceded) government student grants in making university
accessible to those of intellectual promise but of modest means.

---

171   p19 RM MacIver 1968 **As a Tale That Is Told** *Chicago.*
172   N Entwistle 1981 **Styles of Learning and Teaching; an integrated outline of
educational psychology for students, teachers and lecturers** *Chichester.*
173   p21 RM MacIver 1968 **As a Tale That Is Told** *Chicago.*

So MacIver aimed for a university bursary. Such bursaries were the product of university endowments of the 19th century; and they still exist today – but with their relative size and significance ravaged by the inflation of the last 100 years.

And so Maclean, dux of the school in 1897, and his close friend MacIver, dux of the school in 1898, were the first Nicolson pupils to attempt a) to gain direct entry to university and b) to win university bursaries, but without having to spend intermediary years in a mainland school; as their, slightly older, fellow school student Alexander Macdonald of Chapter 3 had done. MacIver and Maclean both succeeded. Aged 16, Robert MacIver took the steamer from Stornoway to Kyle of Lochalsh and then the train on to Edinburgh University. He and Maclean were pioneers on a journey that thousands have since taken. As he crossed the Minch on a blustery September night, MacIver reflected that "*I would never make my home on that island again, beyond my summer visits*".[174] Nor did he.

Robert's narrative about being a student in Edinburgh in 1898 is interesting:

> *I lived in a cheap but quite decently kept rooming house for students. All meals were included, simple but respectable meals – and the whole cost ran to about fourteen shillings a week. Occasionally I would indulge in the luxury of a small hotel near the Old University, and that never cost me more than a shilling.*[175]

So, in a 30-week student year, he was spending £21 a year on board and lodgings. But he had a bursary (see page 53) of £25 to cover this. He also described how the university provided lectures, but regarded itself as having no pastoral or guidance function for students. For 19th century Scottish universities, this was typical; and somewhat different from 19th century Oxbridge. The days of halls of residence, of advisors of study, of university

---

174   p42 RM MacIver 1968 **As a Tale That Is Told** *Chicago.*
175   This and all subsequent quotations in this chapter are from RM MacIver 1968.
As a Tale That Is Told *Chicago* (except where otherwise stated).

health services and so on lay somewhere far ahead. Of the Professor of Greek, he says: *"Although I stood very high in the class, I do not recall ever having an interview with him"*.

He played golf (pennies a round), saw Ellen Terry and Henry Irvine in *The Merchant of Venice* and watched a *D'Oyly Carte* production of *The Mikado*.

MacIver did not work during his summer holiday at home. He played golf with his father at the course in Melbost (now Stornoway Airport) and he studied in preparation for the second year at university. So clearly his bursary, and being in the family home during the long summer vacation, was sufficient to sustain him financially.

MacIver's memoir remind us that university lecture halls in the 19th century could be rowdy places, a tradition which extended, in abated form, at least into the 1960s; but is now dead. And he also observed the rowdiness that could attend rectorial elections, a tradition that has survived.

After an uninspired second year, MacIver in his third year ends up joint first in the logic class. He records the fate of the student who shared the prize:

> *He was killed very early in the hideous folly of the First World War, and of its uncounted victims no one could have been more grievously miscast for soldiering than that gentle scholar.*

MacIver won a further scholarship which he used to take an extra year to ensure a 1st Class Honours; and he duly succeeded in that ambition. Meanwhile he argues with classmates on the significance of the recently deceased Queen Victoria:

> *Some of my pals... shared the general veneration of the queen as a great and wise ruler. I held she was a great symbol... but not great in her own wisdom as a policy-maker.*

MacIver's formal studies at the time may have been classics; but one can see the promise of an ability that would make him a world-renowned social and political analyst.

I was developing a stronger interest in social movements and issues. Much as I felt that I had benefitted from my classical studies, I began to wish that I could enter the unexplored and still academically slighted social sciences.

Robert acquired the coveted first class honours in classics and proceeded to Oriel College Oxford with

a good-sized scholarship masquerading as a Bible clerkship... [and] the obligation of reciting a Latin grace several days a week after the gong had sounded for dinner in the college hall.

What his highly religious presbyterian father back in Stornoway thought of this is not recorded.

MacIver's description of Oxford is of a tranquil life to which he adapted with some ease. His Provost dispensed tea from two teapots, one to provide water to warm the cups (that water then being discarded) and the other for the tea itself. Of the upper class "commoners", as opposed to those like him holding scholarships, he says:

In spite of their greater savoir-faire *I thought of them as more big-boyish, less adult, than our own youth.*

But he records:

The more we studied the social and political life of ancient times, the more eager I was to learn about the doings and the troubles of our own tangled society.

After his Oxford success, Robert MacIver was appointed a lecturer in the University of Aberdeen.

The University of Aberdeen website until recently celebrated that appointment at length and with some pride and humour:

Despite its ancient origins, the University of Aberdeen was one of the first institutions in the UK and further afield to introduce the subject of sociology. In 1907 **Robert MacIver** *(1882–1970), a young lecturer of local birth, was appointed as an assistant in Moral Philosophy but delivered lectures in the new subject.*

*We believe that among his students at that time was the future
father-in-law of the Chinese Communist leader,* **Chairman
Mao**. *Whatever influence Aberdonian sociology had on the
subsequent development of Maoism is unrecorded.*[176]

MacIver initially lectured in political science, *"traditionally
little more than an account of the doctrines of the well-known figures
from Machiavelli to Hegel"* as he put it. He planned however to
write his first book on *"the complicated relationships of men and
groups and of the institutions that had grown up to facilitate control
of these relations"*.

MacIver describes an Aberdeen University that was still 19th
century in its governance: the some seven professors had a say
in that, but no other staff. [177]

Most significantly, he became in 1911 a lecturer in political
science and sociology, the first person to be so designated in a
UK university.

Robert went home for a holiday, probably about 1913. His
father had bought a Model T Ford from the 1911-founded Ford
factory in Trafford Park Manchester; and they both experimented
with driving it. Father MacIver diversified from his Harris Tweed
company into car-hiring; and this was the origin of MacIver's
Garage, a well-known Stornoway company for many decades. At
some point about 1970, I heard for the first time about Robert M
MacIver. I asked my mother whether she knew of him. *"Yes."* she
said, *"Of course he came from MacIver's Garage"*. I understood then,
and still understand today, that a rough translation of this was:

*If one wants to be a world class sociologist, coming from the
family of MacIver's Garage in Stornoway naturally gives one
a distinct head start.*

---

176   http://www.abdn.ac.uk/sociology/history/accessed on 31/12/2011.
177   GE Davie 2013 **The Democratic Intellect: Scotland and Her Universities in
the Nineteenth Century 2nd Edition** *Edinburgh.*
While subject to revisionist onslaughts on some of its interpretations, this remains a
definitive account of the governance and functioning of 19th century Scottish universities.

In his time in Aberdeen the draft of his first book had won a Carnegie award. He got married – to an Aberdonian, Ethel Peterkin.

But he moved on. He was appointed in 1915 to a post in political science in Toronto. So MacIver left the University of Aberdeen – resulting also in the end, for some decades, of any teaching of sociology in that university.

Temporarily leaving his pregnant wife and his first child behind, Robert sailed for the New World, a journey he regarded as a permanent migration. *"I had no expectation of ever remigrating to my native land"*.

The Canadian years saw MacIver: become a well-regarded author; begin to establish himself as someone who could be called upon by governments; and live through a period of thorough disillusionment with the post-War world.

His first book was *The Community: A Sociological Study* (1917) well received by most, apart from a review by Robert E Park – then one of the world's foremost sociologists. The praise from the many counted less for MacIver than the criticism from Park. However, beneath MacIver's benign manner, there seems to have been a trait of steel which manifested itself at several points in his life: he attributes Park's views as much to a Park defect as to a MacIver inadequacy.

There followed *Elements of Social Science* (1921), a book *"of modest, thin, back-street longevity"* in the words of the author. It may indeed have been modest but it contains one of his best known quotations; and one which explains why MacIver did not always endear himself to American sociologists of the subsequent decades – who were often dedicated, first, to the pursuit of the empirical rather than the philosophical; and, second, to the strict measurement of social data.

> *We are apt to think we know what time is because we can measure it, but no sooner do we reflect upon it than that illusion goes. So it appears that the range of the measureable is not the range of the knowable. There are things we can measure, like time,*

*but yet our minds do not grasp their meaning. There are things
we cannot measure, like happiness or pain, and yet their meaning
is perfectly clear to us.*[178]

In 1927, he migrated from Canada to the United States
to become head of department at a college of the University
of Columbia. *"On a September morning we all arrived in New
York, to make, as it turned out, the United States our homeland ever
thereafter"*. His journey from Stornoway to New York had been
a long one chronologically (1898 to 1927); and academically and
psychologically. He remained in the University of Columbia for
some 23 years, for most of that time being professor of political
philosophy and sociology.

Some 10 years after going to the USA, Robert revisited his
native island. This is chronicled in a contemporary essay which he
later appended to his 1968 autobiography. So what did the great
sociologist, and one who specialised in the idea of "community",
make of Lewis in the 1930s? He writes well and yet with deceptive
simplicity, his prose verging on poetry. As a description of
Stornoway in the early 20th century and as a recollection of
teenage life there in the 1890s, it is hard to surpass:

> *How unchanged the little town seems, especially to those who
> come from the changeful world without. The same kippering
> sheds, the same barrels and herring troughs, the same quays,
> the tides still ebbing and flowing between the same walls, the
> little boys still fishing off the same stone steps... the same sombre
> religion, just as the same tides come up the bay. The traveller
> feels, perhaps with surprise, how deep are the roots of that life
> and custom from which he has gone apart. He has changed, but
> it abides.*
>
> *Here the spur of ambition first urged me to strive towards
> dawning goals. Here I was nursed in the strong uncomfortable
> language of heaven and hell, offering the oppressive alternatives*

178   http://todayinsci.com/M/Maciver_Robert/MaciverRobert-Quotations.htm
Accessed 27/8/2015.

of lurid damnation and meaningless bliss, and shook myself free at length, with vast relief, from their ancient spell. Here I learned, from the silent starry nights, the immutable eternity of law that rings about our little lives. Here I heard the secret voice of nature, borne through the winds and the waves, telling of life and death. Here lived my comrades and first friends, my rivals and boyish foes. Here was my home, where a father toiled for me and a mother watched over me with indomitable love. And here the light shining in the eyes of a girl first stirred profounder deeps, as an angel might descend to trouble the pool, and left me alone and wondering, subdued by a breathless, fearful joy.

Such a land has bred its own people. Where the earth yields so little to their toil, men must follow the sea as well. A grave and patient race, they are content with little. They wring meagre crops of oats and potatoes from their crofts, and eke them out with the precious harvests of the sea. Precarious in another sense as well, for the sea is never to be trusted, and every village nurses the tragedy of the men... and the boats that do not return.

This people is much-enduring and sombre-minded. They have few comforts and few recreations, and even the latter incline to melancholy. Their native songs are for the most part minor and plaintive, telling of far dreams and ancient yearning, of parted love and eternal farewell...

His characterisation of Lewis religion is a bleak one. As is his judgment of its effects on local culture:

It holds the quintessence of this religious spirit, which has none of the boisterous joy in salvation evinced, for example, by the east coast fishermen or the blithe sense of liberation from sin that, for example, the Salvation Army proclaims...

It regards art and beauty as lures of the devil or at best as profane pursuits unworthy of the seriousness of life.

One can understand why Professor MacIver, despite his renown, did not endear himself to the community from which he had arisen.

It was his last visit to Lewis.

A measure of MacIver's standing by now was his receiving an honorary degree from Harvard University in 1936. He was included in a *"roster of scholars, drawn from countries across the world, who were recipients of this recognition during the tercentenary of Harvard."* He refers *en passant* to having an honorary degree already – from Columbia.

Through these years there were ongoing tensions between Robert MacIver and a man he himself had head-hunted, Robert Lynd. Lynd had been recruited largely on the basis of a, still well-regarded, book "Middletown", a study of a small (30,000) USA town. Given that Robert's central interests also revolved around the concept of "community", one might have expected the two Roberts to get on well with each other. But this proved not to be the case. Lynd had a more starkly utilitarian view of the study of sociology than did MacIver. And Robert Lynd tended to side with the young academics who favoured a more statistically based methodology within the department.

A vacancy occurred in the department in 1941. MacIver favoured appointing Robert K Merton whom he regarded as *"the most promising of the younger sociologists"*; Lynd favoured Paul Lazarsfeld, a more statistically-oriented scholar. In a classic academic compromise, both were appointed. Ironically, Robert K Merton (1910–2003) and Paul Lazarsfeld (1901–1976) are both today better remembered in the world-wide academic community of social scientists than is either one of the (other) two Roberts. By 1950, Lazarsfeld and Merton were indeed both stars; but Robert MacIver regretted that it was the philosophy of the former that largely dominated and shaped the Columbia sociology department.

Robert MacIver had passed the peak of his intellectual eminence as a sociologist. The world of sociology became – and remains to this day – one that is largely dominated by approaches to data gathering and to data analysis towards which MacIver was not well disposed.

Aged 68 in 1950, MacIver approached the age of compulsory retirement. This was not a prospect he relished. On retirement, he made a sideways shift from full-time sociologist into a part-time post in political theory and governance.[179] And he became involved in a whole variety of public projects, many of them about the governance of public organisations.

He writes amusingly about receiving, on his last visit to Scotland in 1952, an honorary degree from his alma mater the University of Edinburgh:

> *At Edinburgh one was expected to show up for the occasion in the cutaway coat and striped trousers of 'morning dress' and don before the ceremony the magnificent scarlet rob of the doctorate. The conferment itself was conducted in an atmosphere of sonorous solemnity and followed by a stately service in St Giles Cathedral. In the evening one sat on a dais at a full-dress banquet surrounded by university leaders and city dignitaries in official regalia. There was a series of toasts beginning with queen and country proposed in short style and witty speeches as the wine went round.*

But he clearly enjoyed it:

> *Without being a devotee of ceremony, I felt it accented the significance of the occasion and made me sense more fully the honour that was being bestowed on me by a great historical institution.*

The same university in 2008 bestowed an honorary degree on Robert MacIver's fellow-islander: Matthew MacIver. The two are related, although not closely. In 1952, when Robert collected his degree, the incoming Chancellor-designate of the University of Edinburgh was HRH Prince Philip. And in 2008, when Matthew

---

179   For a brief but useful summary of MacIver's own political theory, see pp. 24–25 EM Burns 1963 **Ideas in Conflict** *London*.

collected his degree, Prince Philip still held the same office. They also appear to be the only two MacIvers ever to have been awarded an honorary degree by Edinburgh. We suspect that both of them were unaware of a third Lewisman (JL Robertson) having – in 1912 – received a similar award from the same university (see page 15).

The University of Aberdeen in 2007 celebrated the centenary of its appointment of Robert MacIver. A 21st century professor of sociology there has written *inter alia*:

> *MacIver was President of the American Sociological Association in 1940... received numerous prizes for his publications and was awarded eight honorary degrees. He was the author of nearly twenty books in a period when publishing was not a full time occupation in the academy. For a time these works became some of the standard texts in sociology.*

> *MacIver's sociological work shows a fascination with the relationship between individuals and society, between individual autonomy and tight-knit communities, or put another way, the compatibility of individualism and strong social organization. He portrayed societies as evolving from highly communal societies to states and saw that these higher forms of social organization needed to retain deep roots in the former. These were enduring themes in early sociology as observers wrestled with the nature of the social bond within the context of emerging individual freedoms and rights and as they sought to conceptualize the evident changes occurring in the nature of social organization... It may well be that MacIver's sociological writings are shaped by Stornoway as mediated through urban Toronto and up-town New York, in that his personal acquaintance with close knit communal life in the Western Isles and the individualized living of an urban metropolis may have given him particular insights into the relationship between individuals and society.*

... his Scottish upbringing had an enduring impact on his conception of sociology, despite having spent all but four years as a sociologist living and working outside Scotland.[180]

Let us give a last word to the American Sociological Association:

Robert MacIver's greatness lies in part in the breadth of his contributions. In this age of specialization, he distinguished himself in two fields: sociology and political science. He wrote twenty-one books, the last at the age of eighty-six. First and foremost a scholar and writer, he was at various periods of his life a public servant and a university administrator. Always, whatever the office, there was the whole man – erudite and imaginative, brilliant and humane, urbane and autonomous, with passionate convictions and flashes of playful wit.[181]

Robert MacIver died in New York on June 15 1970. He was 88.

---

180   2007 JD Brewer *An Introduction to MacIver at Aberdeen* Proceedings of the Robert Morrison MacIver Centenary Conference University of Aberdeen, 18 May.
181   1971 *The American Sociologist*, February.

7

DONALD MACKENZIE: FROM POINT TO PRINCETON

BY

IAIN SMITH & JOAN FORREST

—

Donald Mackenzie was the 1882 son of a single mother from Aird Point. He successively was: dux of the Nicolson Institute; a first class honours graduate and member of staff of the University of Aberdeen; a church minister; and a professor in Princeton Theological Seminary. To this day there are still folk memories of "Domhnall Seonaid"[182] in the Aird community.

---

182 "Donald, the son of Jessie/Janet". In official English language certification (e.g. birth certificate of her son, in most census data, in her son's marriage certificate), her name is generally rendered as "Janet" – except for the 1891 census where she appears as "Jessie" as she also did in her death certificate in 1918. Our thanks to Bill and Chris Lawson for tracing the 1891 record, which we had failed to spot. When Donald named one of his daughters after his mother, it was the name "Janet" that he used.

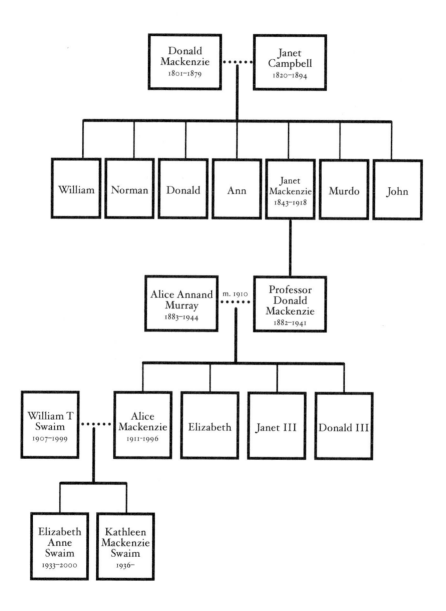

Donald Mackenzie 1801–1879 ···· Janet Campbell 1820–1894

William | Norman | Donald | Ann | Janet Mackenzie 1843–1918 | Murdo | John

Alice Annand Murray 1883–1944 — m. 1910 — Professor Donald Mackenzie 1882–1941

William T Swaim 1907–1999 ···· Alice Mackenzie 1911–1996 | Elizabeth | Janet III | Donald III

Elizabeth Anne Swaim 1933–2000 | Kathleen Mackenzie Swaim 1936–

Professor Donald Mackenzie is seen in a photograph in the 1973 Nicolson Institute centenary school magazine as a man of some gravitas: a watch chain adorns his slightly straining waistcoat and through his rimless glasses he gazes at us with a solemn but kindly beam.

He is recorded in his 1942 Princeton obituary as having been born in the Island of Lewis on 30 May 1882. And there is indeed a birth certificate, one only, which matches that. It records the birth on 30 May 1882 of a Donald Mackenzie in "Aird, Point, Stornoway" to an unmarried Janet Mackenzie, a "Domestic Servant". Janet Mackenzie's own parents were a Donald Mackenzie and a Janet Mackenzie (née Campbell) of 5 Aird Point.[183]

Now hang on to these names, dear reader: for, in typical Hebridean style of the last two centuries, simple names are repeated from generation to generation.

Janet Mackenzie (1843–1918) was illiterate, judging by the "her X mark" on her son's birth certificate. Unusually for a single mother both then and today, Janet (junior) was 39 years old when her only known son was born. She did not ever marry. There is a recent, and otherwise admirable, publication in which she is described as having been "mentally handicapped";[184] but such judgments at that time were highly subjective, and often moral rather than clinical. There were no clinical instruments in the 19th century to assess the presence or extent of what we would now typically call "learning disabilities".

We have recently come across somebody who recollects hearing the story of Donald and his mother in the 1940s; and remembers Janet being referred to as *Seonaid Bochd* ("Poor Janet"). So, all in all, Donald had a somewhat inauspicious and slightly mysterious start in life.

---

183   Donald is described in some publications, notably in the USA, as "Donald Campbell Mackenzie". And a surviving granddaughter has referred to him frequently in conversation with us as "DCM".

184   p125 C Ferguson 2003 **Children of the Black House** *Edinburgh.*

His widow recalled:

At four he was tossed fully dressed into the Atlantic by some teasing schoolboys and, to his great amazement, found he could swim, an accomplishment he enjoyed almost to the end of his life.[185]

In the 1891 census, we find the 9-yr-old Donald resident in Aird with his mother and grandmother, both monolingual Gaelic speakers – as was common for those whose early years preceded the 1872 Education Act. Donald himself is a bilingual "scholar" in the local Aird elementary school where Angus Macdonald is headteacher and his sister Jessie Macdonald is an assistant schoolmistress.

And Donald was certainly some scholar. For, at a time when most of his classmates left school at 13 to work on the croft or in fishing, Donald instead migrated to secondary "higher grade" education in Stornoway (about 1894 and with a Council bursary).[186]

Secondary post-elementary education had been created in the Nicolson Institute, as we have seen, only a little time before he arrived there.

There is an 1898 record of several pupils receiving a Merit Certificate (awarded for high performance to pupils over the age of 13 i.e. post-elementary secondary students): one was D Mackenzie.[187] We are reasonably sure that that was him.

Donald Mackenzie was dux and classics medallist of the Nicolson Institute in 1900.[188] He passed the Arts Preliminary Exam for the University of Aberdeen[189] and went on to the University of Aberdeen 1901–1905, certainly having won a Ross-shire County bursary[190] of £25 per year for three years.[191] At 2014

185   p1 Mackenzie archive in Stornoway Museum Ref No. A2016/006/1.
186   1897–98 Nicolson School Report.
187   Nicolson Institute school log.
188   See page 53 of Chapter 4.
189   Nicolson Institute school log October 19th 1900.
190   August 1899 School Board minute. Third-placed in a Highland-wide competition.
191   p6 1999 **The Nicolson Institute 125th Anniversary Magazine** *Stornoway.*

prices that is about £2750 per year. And he had his university tuition fees, perhaps £500 per year at 2014 prices, paid from a new source of support – as his wife recollected:

> *The Mackenzie family, père and mère, will always look on him [Andrew Carnegie] as a benefactor, for his Scottish University tuition scheme first came into force the very year both entered college, and for both these four years were happier and fuller just because he had lived. In such strange ways are individuals as far apart as Andrew Carnegie of Pittsburgh and Donald Mackenzie of Lewis bound up together in God's bundle of life.[192]*

It took many more years before any other single parent child achieved such progress in the Nicolson Institute.

As we have seen from the very start of this volume, Scottish stories of poor late 19th century rural boys of talent making good despite lowly beginnings are common, but largely mythical. There were indeed such cases; but they were few in number. Donald's slightly older fellow school students Robert M MacIver and Donald Maclean were talented but hardly, as we have seen in Chapter 4, of low beginnings. Donald Mackenzie is in danger of adding to the myth, for he (very exceptionally) bucked the general trend:[193] by the March 1901 census, he is a bilingual 1st year "arts student" and "boarder" from "Ross-shire, Stornoway" in Rosemount Place in Aberdeen.

Mackenzie is a good illustration of a quotation from Professor Devine which we have already cited (on page 3).

> *There were enough real examples, though untypical, to give credibility to the myth, especially when Carnegie grants for university study were established from the early twentieth century.*

---

192   p16 Mackenzie archive in Stornoway Museum Ref No. A2016/006/1.
193   RD Anderson 1983 **Education & Opportunity in Victorian Scotland** *Edinburgh* is the classic work on the general trend.

Mackenzie was active in the Celtic Society at university.
He graduated in 1905 with 1st class honours in philosophy; and
lectured there in logic and metaphysics from 1906 to 1909. So he
was a contemporary on the Aberdeen staff of his fellow-islander
Robert M MacIver but MacIver's autobiography makes no
mention of this: they were both young Lewis men, but of different
backgrounds and of increasingly divergent views. For Mackenzie,
study in the German cities of Halle and Berlin (which made him
a fluent German speaker) preceded a year at the Aberdeen United
Free Church College where he was "the most brilliant student
of his year, standing first in the all-Scotland exit examination" as
records his wife;[194] and he was ordained in 1910.

In 1910 Donald Mackenzie married. His marriage certificate
records his parents as having been a "deceased builder" Donald
Mackenzie and a Janet Mackenzie née Campbell: she is notably
not recorded as "deceased". So Mackenzie gave his grandparents'
names on his marriage certificate as being his parents. Nor
was this a genuine mistake, as it often is when a single parent
child is raised by grandparents, especially when the mother is
presented as an older sibling: for Mackenzie had not been raised
by his grandparents. It was, for highly understandable reasons,
deliberate obfuscation. Donald Mackenzie senior, grandfather,
had died 3 years before his grandchild was even born; and Janet
Mackenzie née Campbell (i.e. Janet Mackenzie senior) had died in
1894: both facts that their profoundly acute grandson would have
known well.

For marriage certificate purposes the living Janet Mackenzie
junior had in effect been given the persona of her dead mother.
Professor Mackenzie had conspired in what the 21st century
calls "identity theft". In his case it was, as far as one can tell, a
victimless crime. But then he was a theologian – so he would have
known that.

Professor Donald Mackenzie's 1910 bride was Alice Annand
Murray, a 27-yr-old "Lecturer in Science" in Aberdeen on the

---

194   p4 Mackenzie archive in Stornoway Museum Ref No. A2016/006/1.

marriage certificate. She was a mathematics graduate of the University of Aberdeen, a granddaughter thinks.[195] As does the US biographer of one of her children. Her late father had been a "Presbyterian Church Minister" who had worked in an overseas mission more than a quarter of a century earlier.[196]

In the 1911 census, there are four inhabited houses at 5 Aird. One of them has a sole and "single" (i.e. unmarried) occupant of "private means": Janet Mackenzie mother of Donald lives there aged 68. Next door to her live her brother Murdo – "shoemaker", his wife Effie, their three adult "fishworker" daughters and their 20-yr-old fisherman son. Their house has 4 rooms.[197]

In the same census in a 10-roomed house in Craigdam Aberdeenshire live Donald Mackenzie the United Free minister, his wife Alice Annand ("Birthplace: New Hebrides, Australasia"; "Nationality: Sch [sic] by parentage"), his mother-in-law and a servant. Donald Mackenzie, having spent his childhood in a very modest house, must have enjoyed the space.[198]

Over the subsequent 18 years, Donald Mackenzie was minister successively in Scottish parishes in Craigdam, Oban, Tain, spending some 10 years from 1916 there, and Ferryhill, Aberdeen.

The minister from the old Hebrides and the wife from the New Hebrides began a family: their first daughter Alice was born in Craigdam on 5 June 1911. The mother subsequently recollected:

> [Mackenzie] *had great fun trying out some student theories and even had his first-born speaking clearly and intelligibly at nine months, and composing complete sentences at little over a year.*[199]

Alice had a childhood, according to her husband's subsequent account, in

---

195   Note from Professor Swaim, her granddaughter, 10/07/2015.
196   In the New Hebrides. He died young in Australia as a consequence of a tropical disease.
197   1911 census data.
198   1911 census data.
199   p8 Mackenzie archive in Stornoway Museum Ref No. A2016/006/1.

a cultural environment extraordinaire... traveling in Europe...
studying the cities, cathedrals and museums.

Seldom did a poetically inclined child ever set forth on life's
voyage on a calmer sea than Alice did, nor with more intellectual
and cultural sails set higher and in the right direction.[200]

So Mackenzie provided his daughter with a childhood that
was in very marked contrast to his own. Two other daughters and
a son were to follow. The son inevitably was called Donald. And
one of the daughters, equally inevitably, was called Janet.

We know from family sources and from the Mackenzie
archive in the Stornoway museum that by 1913 Janet Mackenzie
had come to spend her dying years with her son. However it was
back at 5 Aird Point that she died on 19th March 1918; and the
death certificate, with the record emanating from her brother
Murdo, is clear that she was a single woman.[201]

Mackenzie was no ordinary pastor. In 1914 he published a
weighty piece "Libertarianism and Necessitarianism" in Volume
VII of the Edinburgh-published "Encyclopaedia of Religion and
Ethics". He is recorded as being a minister in Oban. And he had
previously published in the same outlet in 1912 while minister at
Craigdam.

In 1916, he used his German expertise to act as an interpreter
in France for captured German soldiers, returning to his Tain
parish by 1919.

In 1927 he was invited to give a series of five lectures on
'Christian Belief and Christian Practice' in Pittsburgh in the then
Western Theological Seminary, a Presbyterian foundation dating
back to at least 1825. And we can trace his voyage to his lecture
commitments in some detail. Donald Mackenzie, "clergyman"
according to the ship's manifest, sailed out from Liverpool to
New York on 11 February 1927 on the Cunard ship *Alaunia*.
Another record of that time says:

200   p193 J Prescott 2008 **A Poet for the Ages: Alice Mackenzie Swaim** *Indiana*.
201   Accessed 15/9/16.

With his wide learning and accurate scholarship, he combines
humor and interest in everyday life. His geniality quickly won
the hearts of his audience which steadily grew larger as the
course proceeded.[202]

This rapidly led to a new job, a new country and indeed a
new continent. For by January 1928 he was "Professor-elect of
Systematic Theology" at the Western Theological Seminary, as its
student prospectus for the forthcoming 1928-29 session recorded.

On 27 July 1928, now 46 years old, he embarks in London
on the *American Shipper* heading for the port of New York.
The term "Professor-elect of Systematic Theology" clearly gave
the shipping line, American Merchant Lines, some problems.
On the ship's manifest they simply, and delightfully, recorded
his occupation as "missionary".

As he was; but perhaps one of the first to be called
"Professor" by a set of natives before he had even come to settle
among them.

With him went on the same voyage:

"Alica A" Mackenzie, 44-yr-old wife, now moving to her third
continent;

Alice Mackenzie, daughter, now aged 16;

Elizabeth Mackenzie, daughter aged 15;

Janet Mackenzie, the third in our little story, daughter aged
11; and

Donald Mackenzie, also the third in our story, son aged 8.

Western Theological Seminary in Pittsburgh had an
elegant quadrangle and a library with 44,000 books. Professor
Mackenzie liked the place; and the place liked him. His obituary
says:

---

202   p49 *The Princeton Seminary Bulletin*, 1942.

During his tenure of this post – from 1928 to 1933 – he won
distinction not only as a teacher, but also as a preacher, a lecturer,
an author and a leader in religious conferences.[203]

In 1934, the same year in which the University of Aberdeen
awarded him the degree of Doctor of Divinity, Donald Mackenzie
was head-hunted at a second attempt to become Professor of Biblical
Theology at Princeton Seminary.

Professor Donald Mackenzie died there on 19th October 1941
aged 59. There is an extensive 1942 obituary of him in *The Princeton*
Seminary Bulletin.

His widow kept many tributes to him, including one labelled
"From a Scottish Brother Minister and Boyhood Friend":

You know Donald was the first to bring great honour to our
village, and that by his own unaided efforts, by his own ability and
determination; and to us boys he was almost a legendary figure.[204]

His eldest daughter was a well-regarded American poet Alice
Mackenzie Swaim. She had been educated in Scotland at Tain Royal
Academy – and then from the age of 17 in Pennsylvania.

If Mackenzie had "a love of words", his daughter certainly also
had:

The hardest thing in the world for me to understand is boredom.
My universe has always been too stimulating... too many sights and
sounds and smells, too much to touch and taste and feel, too much to
remember, and at times, alas, too much to forget.[205]

One memoir records:

Although her poetic career did not begin until she was about 36 years
of age, she became world renowned, earning prestigious awards
such as Poet-Laureate of the Sonnet and Scottish-American
Poet-Laureate. She received more than 800 poetry awards, was
recognized in approximately 35 Who's Who's [sic], including The

---

203   p49 *The Princeton Seminary Bulletin*, 1942.
204   p35 Mackenzie archive in Stornoway Museum Ref No. A2016/006/1.
205   p10 J Prescott 2008 **A Poet for the Ages: Alice Mackenzie Swaim** *Indiana*

World's Who's Who of Women, Who's Who of American Women and International Who's Who in Poetry. It has been reported that she published more than 8000 poems.[206]

Her most-quoted verse reads:

Courage is not the towering oak

That sees storms come and go

It is the fragile blossom

That opens in the snow.[207]

Her father Professor Mackenzie had lived long enough to see two grandchildren born to daughter Alice: Elizabeth Anne Swaim in 1933 and Kathleen Mackenzie Swaim in 1936. Elizabeth retired as Rare Books Librarian and Archivist at the Wesleyan University Library Middletown, Connecticut. She died on May 15 2000.

Kathleen, who just remembers her maternal grandparents, earned a PhD in 1966 and retired in 1999 from the University of Massachusetts/Amherst as Professor of English, where her specialism was Milton.

Professor Swaim lives in Wendell Massachusetts; and has been kind and informative in adding to our narration of the story of her maternal grandfather. She has also lodged an archive of his and his wife's papers in the new (1916) Stornoway museum.

What Janet Mackenzie the illiterate, single and (allegedly) "mentally handicapped" mother from Aird would have made of the success of her progeny we do not know. We like to think that she would have been proud.

---

206   http://www.findagrave.com/cgi-bin/fg.cgi?page=gr&GRid=43026839
Accessed 28/8/2015.
207   http://balancedwomensblog.com/courage-by-alice-mackenzie-swaim/
Accessed 28/8/2015.

8

JOHN MUNRO,
THE LOST GAELIC POET

BY

Iain Smith & Ruairidh Maciver

———

"Who would not sing for Lycidas?" – Milton.
It is said that teachers cried in the Nicolson
Institute staffroom in 1918 when they heard of the
death of John Munro. They were used to the death
of ex-students by then. But thought the loss of
Munro particularly poignant.

John Munro ("Iain Beag" or "Iain Rothach") son of a fisherman was born in 1889 in Swordale and raised in Aignish, an adjoining village in the Island of Lewis. He was educated at the local school.

The teenage John Munro initially chose to stay on in that 'elementary' school as a pupil teacher. As we have seen in Chapters 1 and 4, it was a role in a teacher apprenticeship scheme of 19th century Scotland: it consistently in the late 19th century gave poor but able students a moderately secure financial route to a teacher training college; and is probably underestimated by some social historians. As we have noted at several points, stories of poor 19th century working class Highland lads equipped only with a formidable intellect and with a sack of oatmeal heading to university in Edinburgh or in Glasgow are mostly that: rather isolated stories. A much more assured road was the teacher apprenticeship. The scheme was however phased out from 1906 before Munro could complete it; and he therefore went to spend three years (1908–1911) in the 'higher grade' Nicolson Institute in Stornoway.

Munro decided that he wanted to go to university, still with a school teaching career in mind: the growth of 'higher grade' education and the 1901-founded Carnegie Trust had by then, as we have seen, made university access for poor but talented students more feasible than it had been for much of the 19th century.

Shortly after Munro's arrival, the Nicolson rector, the nationally famous WG Gibson, set up a school poetry competition. Munro chose the Isle of Lewis as his theme and composed an ode in blank verse. His schoolmate Murdo Murray[208] tells us that there was an external adjudicator for this

---

208 Murdo Murray whom we have noted earlier (p55) was born in 1890, the son of a shoe-maker; Nicolson Institute dux of 1909; and graduate of the University of Aberdeen in 1913. Like his friend Munro he went to war in 1914; like Munro he wrote innovative Gaelic poetry about his war experience; but unlike Munro he survived the Great War. He returned to a teaching career, ultimately as a school inspector, and lived until 1964.

competition, Grierson – who was Professor of English at the University of Edinburgh, a poetry specialist and subsequently tutor to the greatest Gaelic poet of the 20th century: Sorley Maclean. Grierson in his adjudication said that he would be surprised if a better poet than John Munro had ever been born in Lewis.

The John Munro school poem, written in English, was previously thought by most Celtic scholars to be lost: in the 1950s, Murdo Murray recorded it in a 1950s issue of 'Gairm' (an academic Gaelic journal, now defunct) as lost; and Gaelic academia accepted his mid-1950s verdict. However, sometime in the late 1950s or very early 1960s, Murray was sent a copy of the "lost" English poem by the daughter of WJ Gibson. As we have discovered, by serendipity rather than scholarship, that copy was reprinted in the 1963 Nicolson Institute magazine and has survived in the school archives. There it is topped and tailed by some interesting notes:

> *The following ode on "Lewis" was written as a school exercise by the late John Munro (Dux 1911, killed in France 1918). Miss Jane Gibson[209] made this copy [and] writes 'I doubt whether many schoolboys nowadays have ever tried to write Miltonic verse; and that... in itself gives this poem almost a historic interest'.*
>
> *We are indebted to Mr Murdo Murray, H.M.I.S. (retired) for sending us the poem.*

It is worth quoting a few – and these are just a few – of the extant lines from Munro, the 18/19-yr-old school Milton. He clearly had some geological understanding of the origins and scarring of Lewisian gneiss:

---

209 See page 62.

A grand old isle washed by the ocean grey.

A fitter theme it were for Homer's harp

Or Vergil's song – to sing the lands that first

From peaceful rest beneath a shoreless deep

Upreared brave forms into a world of waste!

Thou had'st a Homer of thine own, my Isle:

Blind Rodrick's harp struck happy strains

But these to thee were lost...

What wonder tho' thy hills be weather worn,

And surface bare of blooming trees, until

Th' unfeeling, thoughtless ever, call thee bleak?

Know they the sorrows that have o'er thee passed?

The scars thou bear'st to show how thou has felt

The grind of grating ice, ton upon ton

And oceans broad, that capped the long gone world?[210]

On reading this, one understands why in the Nicolson Institute of 1963 there still remained oral folk memories of John Munro. Even the oldest teachers in 1963 had of course not taught Munro. But some could recall the memories of senior colleagues of the 1930s: who remembered Munro as the ablest of school students; and who remembered also the tears in the staffroom in April 1918. This was in a school where staff did not easily shed tears, then or now.

After three years in the Nicolson Institute, having gained the Higher Leaving Certificate and been awarded the school dux medal, John Munro went to university, probably with a Carnegie scholarship. Graduating from Aberdeen University in

---

210   Nicolson Institute archives: **1963 School magazine.**

1914, he by then planned to train for the Free Church of Scotland ministry, but these plans were put on hold with the outbreak of war. He enlisted immediately as so many did – for reasons that remain speculative even to such an imaginative historian as Niall Ferguson[211]; and served in France with the Seaforth Highlanders from 1914.

A 1920 source, now in public record, says:

> *When war broke out in August, he volunteered and joined the 4th Seaforths. He was sent to France about the end of 1914, and served there continuously but for the short period he was in training at Gales Camp for his commission[212]. During these years, he was in many engagements with the enemy and had many miraculous escapes, till the fateful day, 16 April [1918], when his beautiful and promising life was ended.*
>
> *He had something to say, from dire personal experience, of nearly every name of sinister import over there: Ypres, Neuve Chapelle, Festubert, Loos, La Bassee, Delville Wood, Beaumont-Hamel, Cambrai, the Somme. And yet though he had seen all and suffered many of the miseries of war, he had come out of it all with his fine body unscathed and his finer spirit unclouded.[213]*

Munro, in the same manner as the soldier-poet Wilfred Owen, was killed in action during the last year of the conflict. Both Munro and Owen were second lieutenants when they were killed; and both were awarded the Military Cross shortly before they died.

For the issue of why Munro and Owen – both of modest origins – were lieutenants, one has to read Jeremy Paxman[214] and Niall Ferguson. An army whose officer class in 1914 was heavily upper-class had, albeit inadvertently, slaughtered so many of them

---

211   Chapter 12 N Ferguson 1999 **The Pity of War 1914–1918** *London.*
212   Almost certainly Gailes in Ayrshire.
213   1920 **Loyal Lewis Roll of Honour.**
http://tributesmemorial.blogspot.co.uk/2010/12/john-munro-27-aignish.html.
214   pp237–239 J Paxman 2013 **Great Britain's Great War** *London.*

by 1915/16 that it had to talent-spot from among its working-class ordinary soldiers for replacements. In those pre-television days it was a macabre early version of "Britain's Got Talent".

John Munro had a young lady-friend (to use early 20th century English). We have seen extracts of letters, not in the public record, which she wrote to Munro's mother after his death. She quotes from a note received from Munro's commanding officer:

> *The battalion was taking part in a counter attack at Wytschaete on that day 16 April 1918[215] and he was killed while gallantly leading the men of his platoon against a position held by enemy machine guns... I do not know if you heard that he was awarded the Military Cross for the most excellent work done by him during the Somme at the end of March. The notification of this award only appeared three days after his death.[216]*

It would be going too far, certainly in terms of fame, to call John Munro the 'Gaelic Wilfred Owen'; but the similarities are interesting. Only three of his Gaelic war poems, albeit quite extensive ones, are currently known to have survived; but there are believed to have been more in now missing manuscripts. Here are but two verses – in English translation by the late Professor Derick Thomson of Glasgow University – from the surviving poems:

OUR LAND

> *Snow mantle on the mountain peaks,*
>
> *like white hair lie the mist streaks,*
>
> *the runnel and the moor-burn*
>
> *leap and pour*
>
> *tumbling and rumbling down the rough glens*
>
> *that skirt and buttress the high bens;*

---

215   March/April 1918 had seen the last major German offensive of the Great War: an offensive initially successful, but ultimately so unsuccessful that it was probably the key to the November armistice.
216   Personal communication from extant family in Aignish.

antlered stags and red deer

roam the long slopes, heather-dun –

this is the Land of Brave Men,

a hero's land of hill and glen,

this is the Land of Brave Men.

OUR HEROES WHO FELL IN BATTLE

With some of them, when they were alive,

we had our differences, did not see eye to eye.

Ah! They have fallen on the battle-field:

We found them lying, wounded to death –

their unsightly dust was all that was left –

five of them lying, like fingers outstretched,

summoning, guiding,

urging fresh effort upon us,

asking us to press on, together,

as when they fell, advancing,

over the plain of the battle-field.[217]

John Munro can be described as the first modern Gaelic poet: Professor Thomson stated that his work was 'the finest early burgeoning of the "new poetry" of the century' and Dr Finlay Macleod has said that he was 'the first Gaelic poet to use a contemporary style'. Sorley Maclean and George Campbell Hay, both war poets too but much later, are seen as the breakthrough poets from tradition to modernity in the Gaelic poetic tradition; but, twenty years before their work appeared, John Munro was taking Gaelic poetry in a new direction.

---

217   pp 252–3 D Thomson 1974 **An Introduction to Gaelic Poetry** *London.*

If his commanding officer inevitably was terse in his private words of consolation, local contemporaries, as the now-digitised records of 1918 show, were more effusive:

> *Lt Munro was recently home from France on furlough. He had returned to France shortly before the German offensive started. During the first fortnight and before the Germans were brought to a standstill, his parents and friends were very anxious as to his safety; but they received the welcome news that he had come through the ordeal without a scratch.*
>
> *Mr Morrison of the Knock School, under whom Mr Munro served his apprenticeship as pupil teacher and between whom there was a strong mutual attachment, had a letter on Monday, written on the 14ᵗʰ: 'These are anxious times' Munro wrote 'and only strength from God can stand the strain of them. May He be with you all at home and with us here, and let His mercy go forth to us'.*
>
> *On Wednesday, his father received a wire [i.e. telegram] from the Record Office, Perth, informing him that his son, Lt. John Munro, was killed in action on the 16ᵗʰ April. The sad news has cast a gloom over the whole parish.*[218]

John Munro was only one of some 8 million or more service personnel who died world-wide in World War 1; and but one of the 720,000 United Kingdom dead. Some are moderately well-remembered: Raymond Asquith, son of the UK prime minister; John Kipling, son of Rudyard; Jack Cornwell, all of 16 years when killed at the Battle of Jutland and posthumously awarded the Victoria Cross.

Among the best-remembered dead, there are certainly poets, including Wilfred Owen, Rupert Brooke ("If I should die, think only...") and the Canadian John McCrae ("In Flanders fields, the poppies blow...").

John Munro is not remembered in that way. But he has his place in Gaelic literary history.

---

218 http://tributesmemorial.blogspot.co.uk/2010/12/john-munro-27-aignish.html Accessed 21 Aug 2015.

He wrote what turned out to be his own epitaph:

AR GAISGICH A THUIT SNA BLÀIR

S iomadh fear àlainn òg sgairteil,

ait-fhaoilt air chinn a bhlàth-chridh,

tric le ceum daingeann làidir,

ceum aotrom, glan, sàil-ghlan,

dhìrich bràigh nam beann mòra,

chaidh a choinneamh a' bhàis –

tric ga fhaireach' roimh-làimh –

a chaidh suas chum a' bhlàir;

's tha feur glas an-diugh 'fàs

air na dh'fhàg innleachdan nàmh,

innleachdan dhubh-sgrios an nàmh a chòrr dheth.[219]

The English translation is again by Professor Thomson:

Many a handsome man, young, agile, quick of hand,

with gay mien matching warm heart,

who had often climbed, with strong step, light, foot-sure, bright

to the high upland of the great hill,

went to his meeting with death –

often fore-knowing its skaith –

went out to the war:

the green grass grows over

the shreds his enemies' arms

left, when holocaust had had its fill.[220]

John Munro was a good man, a scholar and a soldier. He was also a fine poet.

---

219   p214 R Black (ed.) 1999 **An Tuil: Anthology of Twentieth Century Verse** *Edinburgh.*

220   pp 252–3 D Thomson 1974 **An Introduction to Gaelic Poetry** *London.*

9

MURDO MACDONALD: A MAN OF NO SCHOOL AND OF ALL SCHOOLS

BY

IAIN SMITH WITH MURDO MACLENNAN

———

Murdo (1907–1940) was a postman, a reluctant crofter and a scholar who had never been to school. There were many autodidacts in the UK in first half of the 20th century; but Murdo was an extreme example.

Murdo Macdonald (generally known as "Murdo Crola") died many years before I was born. He lies beside his parents – in the graveyard of the now-deserted island of Scarp.

This is a story that we (Murdo Maclennan and I) know through a combination of oral history, the Uig Historical Society,[221] and various archives.

My father was born in Shawbost in the Outer Hebrides in 1908 to a family that were very poor even by local standards of the time. Their story was well-documented by his younger brother Calum as we have seen in Chapter 5.[222]

But, by 1932 or thereabouts, a combination of his own father's encouragement and a Carnegie scholarship had allowed my father to escape from poverty and he had become a head teacher. So he went to Crowlista in Lewis, 24 years old or so.

In the village he met the church ministers and the doctor who (along with the head teacher) were the entire middle class of an otherwise working class community.

He was however a bit surprised when one church minister said:

> *You must meet Murdo Crola, a local postman, a man who has never been to school. When I first came here, a few years ago, Murdo and I went for a walk along the local cliffs. And, as the sun was sinking in the Western sky on a beautiful evening over the vast expanse of the Atlantic Ocean, I could not help but say two lines from the Odyssey. Murdo said to me 'Yes, minister: the Greeks also loved the sea' and then quoted to me the next two lines.*
>
> *John, this is no ordinary postman.*[223]

My father sought out Murdo Crola the postman and they became friends.

---

221   See http://www.ceuig.com/archives/593. Accessed 27/7/2011.
222   C Smith 2001 **Around the Peat Fire** *Edinburgh*.
223   Murdo may have acquired some of his knowledge of Greek verse from the then minister in Tarbert Harris. Personal communication from Murdo Maclennan.

Crola in Uig on Loch Resort is a very beautiful place; isolated today as much as it was on 13 January 1907 when Murdo was born there. Today some of the houses are still standing, but are deserted.

> *It is more than 5 miles from the nearest road, across a trackless and featureless moor, rimmed by the hills of Uig and Harris. You pass Morsgail Lodge, follow the shore of the loch to a group of ancient beehive huts, and then strike into the moor, with nothing to guide you but the stones set up at intervals by successive postmen as markers in the mist.[224]*

There are several historical descriptions of Crola. Its rationale was, so I was told, some fishing and crofting and it being a place where deep sea trawlers came for shelter and to take on fresh water. One short but interesting account is by the well-known writer Ian R Mitchell.[225]

Why was a child born in 1907 never sent to school, in apparent contravention of the 1872 Act? (The nearest local school at Luachair existed in 1901 but had closed by the time Murdo was of schooling age.) The probable answer: it was very costly for Education Boards to discharge the legal obligations they had inherited from the 1872 Education Act. So, as happened in parts of the Highlands and Islands, his older sister Kate was sent to school – in Scarp:[226] the Board had no choice but to send her to school somewhere – because she had no elder sibling. Kate was given elementary education on Scarp, where she lived with a relation during term time. She was a very good pupil: indeed the little we know about her suggests that she was generally a very talented woman.[227] Then her mother died and Kate returned to Crola to look after her father and her brother.

Kate was designated as Murdo's teacher and given a small stipend; and that satisfied the legal requirements of the 1872 Act.

---

224 James Shaw Grant "In Search of Lewis-177" **Stornoway Gazette** 27th July 1984.
225 **Press and Journal** 1 October 1993.
226 Not in Crola, as some accounts say.
227 see http://www.ceuig.com/archives/593. Accessed 27/7/2011.

Reports from other observers give the same account.[228]

Kate taught her little brother Murdo to read and to write; and he got so enthused about reading that, when the trawlers came into Loch Resort to get fresh water, he begged off them whatever reading material they had.

Crola was, and is, very remote. On Sunday evenings, the walk to the church was across a rough track. By the time Murdo was 7 or 8 years old, his grandmother was too infirm to make the walk. One Sunday, the family went to church to listen to a distinguished visiting preacher. When they got home, Granny inquired "What did the preacher say?" Murdo's parents explained that the preacher had been "very powerful"; but so powerful that the gist of the sermon had passed over their heads. Murdo said "Granny: let me tell you"; and did so. The grandmother allegedly said, at the end of this disquisition:

> *My beloved grandson: you are a child who will either bring great distinction to this family – or great disgrace.*[229]

Murdo grew up, always reading a huge amount. He read religious literature; and became devout about that. He read a huge amount of socialist literature: George Orwell, the New Statesman and publications of the Gollancz Left Book Club; and became devout about that too. He was in some ways typical of aspiring, radical and deprived young people of the 1930s. And he studied other things: certainly English literature. On his visits to Tarbert the minister Dr Macleod took a keen interest in Murdo and would take him to the manse for some tutoring in the classics.[230]

A retrospective 1984 account of Murdo by James Shaw Grant (who in the 1930s and subsequently was editor of the Stornoway Gazette; and who knew Murdo both personally and through his correspondence) says:

---

228 Personal communication from Murdo Maclennan: 28 Feb 2011.
229 The account of this that I inherited from my father and that currently told on the Uig website disagree a bit in detail, but agree in substance.
230 Personal communication from Murdo Maclennan. But Murdo Crola's study of written Greek did not occur until the mid–1930s.

Despite the fact that he had no public schooling, he was widely read, and wrote in a slightly pedantic, but highly intelligent way, on a variety of subjects. He corresponded with many distinguished people – including a number of professors – whom he met while they were fishing at Morsgail, and he sometimes contributed sane, perceptive letters to the 'Stornoway Gazette' [231]

Murdo had acquired a job as the local postman and he worked on the family croft. But, according to my father, Murdo saw the sheep in Crola as part of the burden that kept him from realising his wider ambitions. This lack of interest in husbandry is confirmed by a story (still apparently extant in Hushinish) that says that one day Murdo confessed to his father that he could not find one of their sheep; to which the father said "No, Murdo: that sheep is one we slaughtered and ate a few days ago".[232] Murdo could remember the lines of Burns and Browning and Shakespeare and Shaw; but had less interest in remembering the sheep of Crola.

Nor did he restrict his debates to correspondence to and from Crola. Seemingly he would hold court on visits to Stornoway. When Murdo visited Stornoway he would debate with some of the local gentry in "Stephen's" shop.[233] The shop of RS Stephen, a shop which survived well into the 1970s, was ostensibly about the sale of pens and stationery. It fulfilled a function that has only recently died out in that town: for it may have been partly about commerce, but it was at least equally a place for locals to meet for debates about politics. Its underlying business model is a mystery to those of us living in the 21ˢᵗ century.

Murdo was clear about his ambitions. He wanted to go to university and get a degree. But how could someone who had never been to school get to university? So he addressed his mind to that small problem.

Murdo wrote to the University of Glasgow; and he got a reply explaining that, although the University increasingly used school-

231   James Shaw Grant "In Search of Lewis-177" **Stornoway Gazette** 27th July 1984.
232   Personal communication from Hector Morrison.
233   Personal communication from Murdo Maclennan.

based Highers as a selection device, it still ran a completely separate preliminary entrance examination of its own. Essentially this was a relic of the time in the 19th century, prior to the Higher Leaving Certificate of 1888, when that would have been its main form of selection. (See Chapter 4.) That reply got Murdo thinking.

He and my father kept in touch with each other, loaning each other books and talking about politics; and much else. One day my father was teaching; and, as he looked out the window, he could see Murdo descending off the hillside towards the school. He asked Murdo why he was visiting in working hours, and Murdo said "John, could I come inside and sit at the back of the classroom?" Murdo did that for an hour and then slipped away, having said to my father "I often wondered over the years what it would be like to go to school and be in a classroom".

In 1935 or so, my father left the area for another post. But Murdo and he kept in touch, rendezvousing on occasion in my paternal grandparents' house in Stornoway. They corresponded. My father's letters are lost; but Murdo's letters from 1st July 1935 to 19th April 1939 were preserved by my father; and inherited by me.

In these years, Murdo speculated as to when he might go to university; he wrote Gaelic hymns (for he was no mean Gaelic poet); he did his duties as a postman; and he wrote about the politics of the 1930s, international, national and local.

In the first letter[234] he writes:

> *I can only plead guilty to a charge of culpable neglect in not having written and forwarded books sooner. Nor have I any extenuating circumstances to offer, my only one being that day after day I allowed time and opportunities to slip through my fumbling fingers; a reason which may recall to you Shakespeare's lines 'Oft the excusing of a fault doth make itself the worst by this excuse'.[235]*

---

234 Letter of 1 July 1935.
235 This is a very reasonable paraphrase of a line in **King John**. Act iv. Sc. 2.

Now some lines I find astonishing from a devout Hebridean Presbyterian of the 1930s; a section my father must have found odd and disturbing – my father like most male Hebrideans of his generation hated talking about such things.

Murdo writes:

> *This man, representative of his class, is willing to work as many hours as he can, but he is married to a young wife. If they have ever heard the phrase 'birth control', they probably think it a mid-wifery [sic] practice or... a different term for polygamy. So the little wife has a large brood. She looks an obvious case of malnutrition – our polite term for prolonged starvation. The over-worked father expressed to me the wish that he was still 'on the dole' as it is impossible for him to earn as much as he (previously) received in this manner.*

Then he goes into a more frivolous mode about a religious pamphlet:

> *It may interest you to know that I gave a copy of this to the three Uig ministers (yes, including the Rev 'Windy-Wordy' of orthodox fame). I did not expect to hear any quotations from it in their pulpits. Worse for them – and for us.*

As 1935 moved on, he turned his attention to the General Election – where the local sitting National M.P. was being opposed by a 21-yr-old student, Malcolm K Macmillan. And Murdo was writing letters to the Stornoway Gazette under the name of "Active Citizen", letters that are in the Gazette archive.

Spurred on by his reading of the Daily Herald[236] and the Forward,[237] Murdo argued in his letters that there was too much concentration on statistics and not enough on the underlying misery. Murdo was much obsessed with unemployment and poverty. He writes:

---

236 Labour Party-supporting daily newspaper.
237 Left wing political periodical.

Few people have the imagination to see and the tenderness to feel
that behind the figures of employment schemes lie the pathos of lovers
who cannot marry and the anxiety of mothers who cannot afford
food for their ailing sickly children.[238]

And he quotes Carlyle:

Mournful enough that an honest worker on English soil looks
wistfully for what the horse he is driving is sure of – food and
shelter.[239]

His letters are full of quotations from books. And he explains
why this is so:

Living here in solitude in 'the back o' beyond' the only thing which
makes its loneliness tolerable, at least to me, is that the door of reading
is open to a larger world of fact and imagination.[240]

He celebrates the fact that Malcolm K Macmillan had won the
Western Isles for Labour ("It was the first time I felt consciously
proud of belonging to the Western Isles") but warns against
complacency in future elections.[241]

In 1937, he is engaged in the Glasgow University entrance
examinations:

I got a pass certificate for Gaelic and Greek, but failed, by what
Principal Macgregor tells me was but 'very few marks', in English.
I wrongfully assumed that there would be a range of optional
questions, so I gave but little attention to the prescribed texts... I was
so late in taking up the study of Greek – I didn't know its alphabet
until last September – ... that I had to concentrate mostly on it...
which probably cost me my English Pass.[242, 243]

---

238   Letter of 5th November 1935.
239   This is actually a summary of a paragraph in Chapter 4 of Carlyle's **"Chartism"**
rather than a direct quotation.
240   Letter of 2nd December 1935.
241   As it happened, Macmillan held the seat for 35 years.
242   Letter of 30th November 1937.
243   Principal Macgregor was the Principal of Trinity College, then a semi-autonomous
part of the University of Glasgow.

T7/L

a torn and patched patches pair of Dungarees.
This man, representative of his class, is willing to
work every hour he can, but he married a
young wife. If they ever heard the phrase 'Birth-control"
they think it probably is some mid-wifery practice, or for
all I know, they might think it a different term
for Polygamy. Anyway, the little wife has a large
brood of family. She looks an obvious case of
mal-nutrition — our polite name for prolonged starvation.
The over-worked father, expressed the wish to me that
he was still "on the dole", as it is impossible for him
to earn as much as he received in this manner.
I need hardly remind you that even thus he
received only 3/- a week per head — or mouth rather.
Comment is superfluous!
                    I am enclosing an able
essay on "the Unknown Soldier." It may interest you to
know that I gave a copy of this pamphlet to
the three Uig ministers — Yes including Rev M.
Windy Wordy of orthodox fame; and also the
Rev Duncan Matheson, Barvas.
I did it expect to hear any quotations from
it in their pulpits. Worse for them — and us!
          By-the-way, if you can find out
for me, from Mr. Grant or otherwise, who was my

Letter of 1st July 1935

of preaching is logical essays arguing the need of a necessity of religion. I never hear of a "convert" by his preaching. It is not otherwise in our political understanding. Few men are guided wholly by reasons which can be given. They are controlled, restrained, inspired by reasons deeper than mere reason, in a region beyond argument for ever. You may over-power one with facts and over-whelm him with statistics, but unless his sympathy is gained for the aim you argue for, he is left with a feeling that there is some weapon in his armoury which would break under your guard if only he could lay his hands on it! He is left with the feeling that one of his side could manipulate figures and arrive at an opposite conclusion. I am convinced there is more propaganda value in such sentences as the following to the average elector than in a column of statistics. Take this, for instance from Carlyle :- " Mournful enough that an honest worker on English soil looks wistfully for what the horse he is driving is sure of; food and shelter" or this from Mrs Booth's " In Darkest England". " Some day we may hope, that every honest worker will be as healthily housed, as regularly fed, and as warmly clad as our are our criminal convicts." Few people have the imagination to see and the tenderness to feel that behind a row of figures of Employment returns is the pathos of lovers who can't marry, the anxiety of mothers who can't afford nourishing food for their thin ailing sick children

Letter of 5th November 1935

But by October 1938 he has succeeded:

> *I was successful in my recent Examination. I got 80% and imagine that I lost most of the other 20% through sheer nervousness. Anyway at this stage a Pass is as good to me as 100%. But unfortunately, due to domestic circumstances, I am unable to enter University this year... I feel it with a keener sense of disappointment than I care to give expression to:*

> *But let us cheerful acquiesce*

> *Nor make our scanty pleasures less*

> *By pining at our state.*[244, 245]

Some, but not all, of his interaction with Glasgow University is still verifiable in the archives of the University of Glasgow: my thanks to the University of Glasgow archivists.[246, 247] And there were at least two persons who for many decades remembered Murdo attending the Nicolson Institute in Stornoway to sit these examinations.[248] Murdo was small in stature and Revd Donald Macrae, one time minister in Tarbert Harris, stated that he remembered when he was sitting his exams in the Nicolson Institute that this *"small man in plus fours and smoking a rollup appeared to take the exams with them"*.[249]

It must have been about this time that Murdo struck up an unusual friendship which is documented in the autobiography of

244 Letter of October 1938 (no detailed date).
245 The quotation, unattributed by Murdo, is from Robert Burns (**The Epistle to Davie, a Brother Poet**, January 1785).
246 Personal communication from the archivist (ref: R10/5/5 in the University of Glasgow archive).
247 After his father died Murdo wished to move to Hushinish and purchased an old shed which workmen building the slipway for the crossing to Scarp had used for accommodation. However the Hushinish crofters refused to give him a site. Murdo then had the shed transported to Luachair, very close to Crola; and used it to store books and papers. (This would explain why the University of Glasgow archives record his place of residence as Luachair; but all his letters to my father use Crola as the heading.)
248 Personal communications from two of my cousins.
249 Both the witnesses to Murdo sitting these exams in essence described him as middle-aged. They themselves were then about 16 years old. Murdo was all of 30 years old.

the late and gifted Professor Murdo Ewen Macdonald.[250]

Professor Macdonald tells the story of how Murdo Crola met Professor Terence Bruce Mitford, himself a remarkable man.[251]

> *One summer, walking in North Harris, T.B., as he was affectionately called, lost his way in a thick mist. Literally he bumped into a man approaching from the opposite direction. This indistinct figure turned out to be the Postman who lived in the village of Croleadha* [sic], *arguably the most isolated in the British Isles. When T.B. asked him to direct him on the way to Stornoway, the shadowy stranger in a heavily accented Gaelic accent answered, 'You will never make it in the mist. Come home with me, stay the night, and tomorrow morning I'll act as your guide on the road to Stornoway'. This was the beginning of the most remarkable friendship I have ever known.*

> *That night, before going to bed, T.B., the Oxford scholar classicist, learned to his astonishment that Murdo Macdonald, who had rescued him in the mist, had never been to school. His astonishment rocketed to an astronomic level when he discovered Murdo had acquired a mastery of English, Latin and Greek.*[252] *In Latin 'Caesar in Britain and Belgium' he* [Murdo] *could translate better than his* [T.B.'s] *honours students. In New Testament Greek he was as much at home as he was in Gaelic. More shocking still was the realization that this so-called uneducated crofter knew more about Shakespeare's First Folios than he did.*

> *The friendship which had its origin in the mist, developed into a beautiful one... The Oxford Scholar and the Crofter Postman wrote to each other once a week and exchanged books. One icy*

---

250 M E Macdonald 2008 **PADRE MAC: The Autobiography of the Late Murdo Ewen MacDonald of Harris** *Stornoway*.

251 http://en.wikipedia.org/wiki/Terence_Mitford. Accessed 27/7/2011.

252 This probably dates the encounter as in 1937 or later: for we know that Murdo Crola did not start his formal study of written Greek until 1936.

winter Murdo succumbed to pneumonia. T.B. sank into deep grief.[253]

But if Murdo Crola was a friend of professors, he was no friend of landlords.

In the 1930s, all of Lewis and Harris (bar the parish of Stornoway, at that time an early and unique community trust) was in private ownership. Murdo writes about the Scotts of the local North Harris estate with ferocity and wit:[254]

> *You would have noticed the syrupy exaggeration of eulogistic compliments to the late Lady Sophie Scott by those who think they have a vicarious greatness if a titled lady deigns to notice them. I lived near enough to Amhuinnsuidhe Castle, that fortress of Toryism, to consider a great deal of what was said but very 'artificial' flowers. Lady Scott and her titled husband were by no means bad specimens of their class; but they share the outlook of their class. In every Election since Labour entered the field, their cars and influence were at the disposal of those who favoured 'non-intervention' in the workers' cause.*
>
> *No Unemployment Insurance is paid in respect of any the workers on the Estate. As for their love to [sic] Harris, it is a love for Harris deer and hills more than for Harris people.*
>
> *A few years ago, there was such poverty in Scalpay that 80 families (I think) were supported by Poor Relief. That same year 80 deer carcases were shipped from Amhuinnsuidhe Castle by Sir Sam and his late spouse to their Mayfair friends; nor did I ever hear that her Ladyship ever said: 'Sam, our pals are fairly well off; but there are people in Harris who have no real dinner. What about sending them a feed from off their own Harris hills?*

---

253 This account, written by Professor Macdonald many decades after the events, may have a small element of romantic embellishment in it. As may be true of other sources we have used. The reason given for Murdo's death is certainly in error. But it matches well the evidence of James Shaw Grant – "he corresponded with many distinguished people, – including a number of professors".
254 Letter of 30th November 1935.

And he was baffled by the respect that the Scotts were accorded from some of the community:

> *To speak like this to some Harris folk would appear blasphemy of the first degree. The Scotts love Harris, I am told, yet Harris sends 50 patients a year to Stornoway hospital and Sir Sam's contribution to it is only the average cost of one operation.*
>
> *Lady Sophie has asked for her cremated ashes to be interred in Harris. But was it with the lowly dust of those who doffed caps to her and felt exalted when she smiled at them from the throne of her riding saddle as she rode along? Why, bless your heart, no!*
>
> *It is where a poodle she once had is buried, emblematic of the outlook of her caste, to whom a favourite lapdog is of more importance than the resting-place – dead or alive – of the poor.*

No doubt it would have pleased Murdo that the North Harris Estate has become in large part, albeit 70 years on, a community trust.

Murdo would have been particularly sceptical of the 21st century lines that say:

> *The proprietorship of Sir Edward and Lady Emily Scott, and of the Scott successors at the Castle, was to be a very flourishing and benevolent one. All house-guests were non-paying and whatever fish or game was not used was given away locally.*[255]

Still in radical vein, he advises my father:

> *If you have a shilling to spare, buy Bernard Shaw's 'Intelligent Woman's Guide to Socialism, Capitalism, Sovietism and Fascism'. It is published in the 'Pelican' series of books at 6d each.*[256]

On Shaw's books on political systems, he writes:[257]

---

255 Accessed 8/3/2011 at http://www.celticcastles.com/castles/amhuinnsuidhe/amhuinnsuidhe-castle-html/history.html.

256 Accessed 8/3/2011 at http://www.fantasticfiction.co.uk/s/george-bernard-shaw/intelligent-womans-guide-to-socialism-capitalism-s.htm.

257 Letter of October 1938 (no day specified).

They are typical Shavian wit and apart from their merit as a 'guide'
a copy of them certainly provides more original wit than two copies
of 'Punch' at the same price. To Shaw Socialism means primarily one
thing, quality[258] of income... Some of the aristocracy of Stornoway
would rather have Hitler Lord Provost of Stornoway with all the
Insignia of Office and Goebbels as Town Clerk than that.

The next month,[259] he thanks my father for a parcel of books:

Jeans' 'The Mysterious Universe' I had bought some years ago:
all the rest are new to me.

He then launches into a long disquisition on the materialistic
interpretation of history; and why he thinks it compatible with
Christianity. Among the points he makes to defend the Church,
he says:

My grandfather had ten of a family and none of them was quite
illiterate, because of the small schools founded and supported by
the Church.[260]

And he quotes Browning:

I cannot chain my soul, it will not rest

In its clay prison; this most narrow sphere—

It has strange powers, and feelings, and desires,

Which I cannot account for, nor explain,

But which I stifle not, being bound to trust

All feelings equally—to hear all sides:

Yet I cannot indulge them, and they live,

Referring to some state or life unknown.[261]

---

258   Presumably he meant 'equality'.
259   Letter of 1st November 1938.
260   Prior to the implementation of the 1872 Education (Scotland) Act, this was a main
form of school provision. And there was still disputation in the 20th century – not least
about Uig – as to what, if anything, the 1872 Act improved. See JS Grant reprinted in
"Back in the Day" August 2016.
261   **Pauline** 1832.

He refers to the author AA MacGregor. Alasdair Alpin MacGregor (1899–1970) was a Scottish writer and photographer, known for a large number of travel books. And for denouncing drunkenness in Stornoway, a point on which his Wikipedia entry is very coy:

> MacGregor was forced to be critically realistic about certain aspects of life on the west coast in his book The Western Isles.[262]

Murdo wrote:

> Comrade Macgregor has given an unsolicited testimonial to Messrs Booze Stornoway Ltd. King Alcohol has enough loyal subjects there. But they are not quite such a ragged army as A A Macgregor imagines he saw.[263]

He goes on:

> He and I crossed swords, or pens rather, in the now defunct 'Scots Observer' and he published a full apology. I saw him here one day since, and asked him to tea. He came in and talked like a gramaphone [sic] out of control... I don't think he is a bad sort at the depth [sic] but it would be better if his censor was not so often unemployed.[264]

There are four more letters in 1939. He discusses land reform and religion:

> The Church question in Uig from 1870 was primarily a land question. The Free Church minister did not take the Land League's side; and that was the occasion of the first breach of the Free Church ranks in Uig. They did not know that they were entering the most Tory Church in Scotland, and it would take me too long to enumerate how. It is significant of this connection between both that all the new settlers in Uig, Reef, Ardroil and

---

262 Accessed 8/3/2011 at http://en.wikipedia.org/wiki/Alasdair_Alpin_MacGregor.
263 This comment from the teetotal Murdo was typical of island reactions, even from anti-alcohol Hebrideans, to MacGregor.
264 Compton Mackenzie apparently had very similar opinions of MacGregor.

Carnish are nearly all 'Seceders' [i.e. people who left the
Free Church of Scotland to join the Free Presbyterian
Church].[265, 266, 267]

He writes much about politics, and scathingly about Cripps.
In early 1939 Cripps was expelled from the Labour Party for his
advocacy of a Popular Front with the Communist Party and anti-
appeasement Liberals and Conservatives.

> *What do you think of our Local Branch supporting Sir Stafford
> Cripps? Likely enough, Comrade Cripps is sincere – as sincere as
> Hitler or Cromwell. Only a sincere man is capable of going to
> extremes; but Sir Stafford has never been much of an asset to the
> Labour Party…When I entered the Lochcroistean schoolhouse
> to vote at the Election, I was confronted by a placarded saying
> of his, placed in a prominent place by the National Liberal
> supporters to frighten the electors against the party who
> condoned such a man!*[268]

In September 1939, Murdo took ill, and entered hospital in
Glasgow. On the outbreak of World War II, he was sent home:
this was the policy for all but the most critically ill of hospital
patients – to clear space for anticipated war casualties. Some of
my father's family blamed this for Murdo's subsequent demise,
but I do not think my father held that view. Murdo, my father
believed, had a brain tumour; other sources attribute his death
to an unsuccessful operation for goitre.[269] Back in the hospital in
Stornoway, he wrote his last religious poem – "*Do Lorg 's Do Bhata
Treun*". It was retrieved from under his pillow after he had died.

---

265 Letter of 12th January 1939.
266 There are various views on the Highland Church and land issues. See, for example,
p157 in D Andsell 1998 **The People of the Great Faith** *Stornoway*. A more recent
publication on church history in the Outer Hebrides (J Macleod 2010 **Banner in the
West** *Edinburgh*) makes almost no references to land tenure issues.
267 In 1932, it is recorded that one "Murdo Macdonald, Crola, Kinreasor (sic)"
spent an annual 3/6 on Free Presbyterian publications. Accessed 27/07/2011 at http://
www.fpchurch.org.uk/magazines/fpm/1932/FPM%20-%20April%201932.pdf.
268 Letter of 10th February 1939.
269 Accessed 8/3/2011 at http://www.ceuig.com/archives/2391.

Figure 11 Annabella (1886–1966): Chapter 5
Portrait by son Donald Smith 1926–2014

Figure 12 Fisher girls of Stornoway circa 1953 at the end of an era:
Chapter 5

One of several sketches by Donald Smith (1926–2014), then a student artist. The fisher
girls, being sure the somewhat Bohemian artist was a mainland non-Gaelic speaker,
speculated in Gaelic in front of him about his potential prowess in bed. At the end of his
sketching session, he thanked them in his fluent Lewis Gaelic.

Figure 13 29 Aug 1907 Fraserburgh. Annabella and Murdo get married:
Chapter 5

Figure 14 Iolaire memorial at Holm, Isle of Lewis: Chapter 5

Figure 15 Murdo and Annabella in later years: Chapter 5
Portrait by son Donald Smith (1926–2014)
Courtesy of Jewel Smith & Sandy Scott

Figure 16 1957 Golden Wedding Picture: Chapter 5

Figure 17 Bragar Cemetery: Chapter 5

Figure 18 Professor RM MacIver 1882–1970: Chapter 6

Figure 19 Professor D Mackenzie 1882–1941: Chapter 7

Figure 20 Alice Mackenzie Swaim: Chapter 7

Figure 21 Murdo Murray's story of his schoolmate John Munro:
Chapter 8

Figure 22 Kinlochresort and Crola: Chapter 9

Figure 23 Murdo and friend: Chapter 9

Figure 24 Milnes Bar, Edinburgh: Chapter 10

Figure 25 Interior of Café Royal Edinburgh: Chapter 10

Here is a stanza from it:

Thig aig a lorg seo feartan ur
Tha cumhachd triuir na Trainaid leis
Gu'n tig an truaghan leis on uir
Gu'm faigh e crun nach criochnaich leis
Is ged a rannsaicheadh tu chuis
Cha tuig thu tus a dhiomhaireachd
Ach gabh e, seinnidh tu a chliu
A stigh an Cuirt na Siornuidheachd [270]

Some of the poem translates into English as:

"This rod and valiant staff
Is so capable; so suitable,
The kindness of our God gave it to us,
It is heaven's provision for our perils,
Jesus made it with his cross,
From his travail and from his suffering,
And from the tree of life that branch was given
As a sturdy staff which He provided.

God's grace is the sturdy staff,
Which He gave to us as an inheritance.
It will not lose its effectiveness when your step
Succumbs, and strength departs from you.
It will give youth to old age,
And liberty to the prisoners,

---

270   Accessed 8/3/2011 at http://www.ceuig.com/archives/2391.

It will guide the blind,

To the Land of Light, and they will see there.

This is the staff which gave the victory

To a people whose strength was sapped,

By it the Red Sea was separated,

And they crossed it safely.

The Ark of the Covenant was in the court,

The censer and the pot of manna was in it,

And the rod with new growth,

It was this staff which was crowned with blossoms for you.

This rod and sturdy staff,

Will not yield when it is tested,

It is the sword of God's spirit,

A sharp, definite edge was given it.

And although your enemy surrounds you,

With an army of trials,

You will break through them to victory,

And you who trust in it will receive a prize.[271]

Murdo died in 1940 in the Lewis Hospital, Stornoway, his ambition to go to university unrealised. He was 31 years old. He is buried on Scarp alongside his father and mother. Most of his papers, writing and books remained in Luachair after he died and unfortunately, as the roof disappeared, they were lost.

After Murdo's death, Kate lived alone in the family house, in a dying village, keeping in touch through the radio news, interested

---

271 Translation by Dr RG Maclean.

in everything at home and abroad and as well informed as if she
lived in the heart of a city... although, at last, old age compelled
her to go to live with relatives elsewhere in Harris [in 1961],
leaving the abandoned crofts to be obliterated by the heather, and
the houses to become another memorial to a vanished race...[272]

Murdo was a learned man and a very talented postman.

So what kind of story is this?

Some of the readers of earlier drafts of this chapter have
pointed out that it is a story that, in a slightly different form,
happened across the UK many times in generations long past.
That is true. But few 20th century stories are quite as extreme as
this one: it has been unusual for the last 120 years or more in the
UK to find children who have never been to school.[273]

It is a story that perhaps provides a counter-weight to some of
the other chapters in this book by reminding us of the distinction
between formal and informal education. Murdo may not have
been to school but he was clearly not uneducated. He drew on a
number of sources and it is perhaps worth noting three that were
of considerable significance in the 1920s and 1930s in Crola and
elsewhere in the UK.

1)   The growth of BBC radio broadcasting from 1922
onwards. For Murdo and his sister the "wireless" with its
lead-acid accumulator was an indispensable tool.

> *Reith fought off the politicians' attempts to influence the BBC,*
> *while offering the British people programmes to* **educate***,*
> *inform and entertain.*[274] *(our emphasis)*

2)   The growth and popularisation of the newspaper industry.
The early years of the 20th century had seen an explosive
increase in newspaper sales. Murdo certainly regularly read

---

272   James Shaw Grant "In Search of Lewis-177" **Stornoway Gazette** 27th July 1984.
273   The system of elementary schools set up in Scotland by the 1872 Act took some
time to implement; and in some parts of Scotland, both rural and urban, suffered for
years from widespread truancy. But it is probably safe to say, as we have in Chapter 1,
that these issues had been largely resolved by 1890.
274   http://www.bbc.co.uk/historyofthebbc/research/culture/reith-1
Accessed 20/8/2016.

the *Daily Herald*, a then best-selling daily newspaper.[275] And we have seen that he read periodicals such as the New Statesman.

3)   The phenomenon of cheap but serious books. The Left Book Club was founded by Gollancz and flourished from 1936 onwards. Even more significantly Penguin Books was established in 1935 by Allen Lane.

Across the UK many autodidacts used these sources. Murdo was but an extreme example.

He was an exceptional person. Who died much too young.

---

275   Ironically and amazingly a direct ancestor of the modern-day *Sun*.

10

HECTOR MACIVER:
A BOHEMIAN ON ROSE ST.

Hector was a teacher, a writer, a broadcaster and a critic. He was also a bon viveur of some distinction. Totally outrageous at times, he still captured the hearts and minds of many people who shared few of his views.

Hector MacIver had a reputation that is chronicled in a festschrift.[276] Hector's claim to fame is a slightly curious one. He was a friend and confidant (and drinking companion) of – among others – Hugh MacDiarmid, Dylan Thomas, Louis MacNeice, and Sydney Goodsir Smith. One price for their acquaintance, given that much of it was spent in the Café Royal in Edinburgh, was just possibly the liver cancer that killed him at a comparatively early age. Drinking with Dylan Thomas was never a particularly healthy activity.

Many of us remember great teachers of our school days. However not many of us, as Karl Miller did, signified our debt publicly with a book dedicated to our teacher; and persuaded Muriel Spark, Hugh MacDiarmid, Sorley Maclean, George Mackay Brown and William McIlvanney to contribute to it. The book is still in print forty years later. But then few of us had a teacher who inducted us into journalism by appointing us a joint editor with him of the school magazine; or who introduced us personally to Norman MacCaig and to Hugh MacDiarmid; or who gave to Dylan Thomas some of our teenage poems for comment.

MacIver's ex-pupil Miller wrote in the introduction to that festschrift that it was:

> *published in the honour of Hector MacIver... He was a writer, a broadcaster, a talker, a speaker, and he produced plays. He was a gifted man and a gifted friend... He was not famous in the usual sense, but he made contributions to more than one of the fields under discussion and he did have a kind of fame. It went by word of mouth and seldom reached the newspapers; it was as oral as the world of his origins.*

The most extensive chronicling of Hector MacIver's early days is in a joint autobiography produced by his wife Mary MacIver long after Hector was dead.[277]

---

276   K Miller (Ed) 2008 **Memoirs of a Modern Scotland,** 2nd Edition *London.*
277   The book is out of print, but still readily available. M MacIver 1990 **Pilgrim Souls: History of Mary and Hector MacIver** *Aberdeen.*

Hector was born in the village of Shawbost in the Outer Hebrides in 1910. His father was a merchant; and his mother a teacher, having worked her way through the pupil teacher route.[278] Although MacIver's father later went bankrupt, the family were affluent by the then standards of that village. Indeed I can remember my own father,[279] a little older than Hector and living in the same village, describe the MacIver household as full of books when his own house had none. Hector and his family lived in a slated "white" house, at a time when most of the villagers were in thatched "black" houses.

While they belonged chronologically to different generations, Hector and the Robert MacIver of Chapter 6 were first cousins (i.e. their fathers were brothers) and of similar merchant class backgrounds.

MacIver's account of his childhood is detailed in places and sketchy in others, with little to say about his years in secondary school. It is in places factually inaccurate. There may have been reasons why his older brother Neil went to secondary school in Kingussie but it was certainly not, as MacIver asserts, because the Nicolson Institute in Stornoway was not yet in existence. Later his description of the town of Stornoway as being asleep when the naval yacht *Iolaire* foundered so disastrously on 1 January 1919 outside Stornoway is wrong: there were hundreds on the quayside.

But the picture of his childhood village is fascinating. Among the features he vividly describes are many that even in the 1910s would have seemed inconceivable in lowland Scotland; and that are now in 2017 for the most part long gone even in Shawbost. Some of them vanished in Hector's own lifetime; almost all the remainder have vanished in the half-century since his death; and the surviving few mostly exist in greatly diminished form.

The thatched black houses that he describes, with the fire in the middle of the floor and in winter the cattle at one end of the house had, with the exception of a few preserved as museums,

---

278   As we noted in Chapter 2.
279   The John Smith who appears in Chapter 5 and in Chapter 9.

mostly vanished by the end of the 1960s and certainly all by the 1970s: a retrograde step for those of a romantic mind, a huge step forward for those more concerned with infant mortality and with general domestic comfort. The Viking-descended water-driven mill for the oats and the barley had fallen into disuse long before the 20th century was half old; the cultivation of the oats and the barley which lasted well into the 1970s has now vanished; the digging of the native peat for use as a fuel survives, but at a volume a fraction of what it was a century ago.

The monolingual English-speaking infant teacher with monolingual Gaelic-speaking infants has gone, at least in that stark form: not least because there are very few monolingual Gaelic children entering infant school.

Only MacIver's description of the treacherous Atlantic and of the winter storms powering themselves in from the ocean would be as applicable today as they were almost a century ago.

MacIver writes about the tasks of the village:

> *I began to take an interest in the work of the croft: ploughing, harrowing, planting potatoes, gathering kelp on the seashore, women spinning, men weaving and so on.*[280]

His description of boys of the 1920s stealing autumn turnips from the crofts would have applied, some 30 years later, to the Hebridean village where I was brought up in the 1950s; as would the New Year theft of carts and other agricultural implements which, in the name of celebrations, were dumped in the village pond. Today these customs are dead. The boisterous Hebridean village lads of today, even if they are so minded, have no access to turnips or to carts: they are reduced to the primitive joys of the iPhone.

Aged 12, Hector goes to the Nicolson Institute for his secondary schooling. We have seen that it was 1898 before it sent two pupils direct to university, one of them the first cousin of

---

280   p63 M MacIver 1990 **Pilgrim Souls: History of Mary and Hector MacIver** *Aberdeen.*

Hector. What Hector did in 1922 or so i.e. attend the Nicolson Institute and then in 1927 go directly to university was by then a moderately common pattern – although in the 1920s still not nearly as common as it is today.

MacIver records that he went to Edinburgh University to study English, British History, Moral Philosophy and Fine Art. There he met Norman MacCaig, Sidney Goodsir Smith and Sorley Maclean, the finest Gaelic poet of his age.

A 1930s literary critic wrote of a 1934 Scottish publication which included essays by Hugh MacDiarmid, Neil Gunn and Eric Linklater:

> *one of the best essays was Hector MacIver's piece on the Outer Isles. It seemed to me full of exciting promise and I took it for granted that we should see much more of his writing.*[281]

And a source of the times quotes an extract:

> *In all the Hebrides, Benbecula is the sea's dearest child. That is why the returning tide races so quickly over the sand, hurrying with pouted lips to kiss its shore. And when the night's embraces are over, the sea leaves Benbecula again, like a mother bird going to forage for its young.*[282]

By then MacIver had obtained a teaching job at the prestigious Royal High School in Edinburgh. But he had also become even more set in the activity for which he became most famous (or notorious). In an autobiographical essay, he wrote:

> *How the walls of the Abbotsford or the Café Royal*[283] *or Milne's*

---

281   p78 G Scott-Moncrieff in K Miller (Ed) 2008 **Memoirs of a Modern Scotland**, 2nd Edition *London*.

282   H MacIver 1936 'The Outer Isles' in G Scott-Moncrieff **Scottish Country** *London*.

283   Never having explored any of these hostelries, I dropped into the Café Royal some time ago – purely for research purposes. I ordered a glass of Sauvignon Blanc and six oysters, and admired the stunning internal design. A member of staff said to me "You like this place?" I said "Yes: the service is good, the wine is excellent, the architecture is interesting, the oysters are fine; and I believe that some famous figures have been in here." She looked at me and said "Yes, sir: five years ago Sting was here."

Bar echoed to the talk at this time, on the state of Scotland, as
Chris [Hugh MacDiarmid] *and Sidney* [Goodsir Smith] *and*
I set the Celtic world to rights. Clouds of blue smoke, gallons of
beer and whisky, witty talk – heart to heart –, narrowness and
prejudice flew out of the Abbot door.[284]

The Café Royal in Edinburgh remains largely unchanged to
this day, its rooms haunted by the ghosts of Compton Mackenzie,
Louis MacNeice, Dylan Thomas – and Hector MacIver. It was
there, again according to Karl Miller, that MacIver one night
assaulted the (now forgotten, but then Paxman-like) broadcaster
Gilbert Harding for having called him "a bloody Highlander".

Hector, like many of his literary friends, enjoyed the good life.
Miller wrote:

> *According to MacNeice, he may once have been in the habit of*
> *sending back his lobster to the counter in the Café Royal if he did*
> *not think it came from Lewis – nevertheless the world was his*
> *oyster.*[285]

This is a most unlikely, if fun, story.

Hector had gifts other than teaching and writing and talking.
In a pub on Rose Street, while no Sting, he one night showed
another of his talents. The musicologist Ronald Stevenson
subsequently wrote:

> *Within a few minutes of our meeting, we had got on to Scottish*
> *music and soon he was singing – I remember his pleasant baritone*
> *– songs from his native Isle of Lewis. And very unusual songs:*
> *they were no 'sangs o' the cratur' but strangely serene psalm songs*
> *sung in the Gaelic, with no less than ten, and sometimes more than*
> *a dozen, notes to each syllable. Such long-linked melismas I had*
> *never heard in any other vocal music.*[286]

---

284 p103 in M MacIver 1990 **Pilgrim Souls: History of Mary and Hector
MacIver** *Aberdeen.*
285 p97 K Miller (Ed) 2008 **Memoirs of a Modern Scotland,** 2nd Edition *London.*
286 p189 R Stevenson 2008 in K Miller (Ed) **Memoirs of a Modern Scotland**, 2nd
Edition *London.*

This may be a slight over-exaggeration: melismas, some very extended, are found in Gregorian chant.

A piece about author and poet Louis MacNeice tells us in an aside something of Hector's literary activity (most of which is now lost):

> *MacIver had published on the iniquities of landlordism, the failures of the herring industry, subsidy and the dole, and the collapse of Lord Leverhulme's attempt to set up manufacturing industry on Lewis.*

Hector's friendship led to MacNeice visiting Lewis and staying with Hector's family in Shawbost. This proved a somewhat traumatic event for all concerned:

> *Louis had stayed with my family and me at An Gearraidh Buidhe and was supposed to be travelling with his wife. Actually he was not married! ... More than twenty years after, my family still became virulent when discussing the 'immorality' of his visit.*[287]

A later writer puts it more bluntly:

> *My English teacher, Hector MacIver, was his friend, the dedicatee of 'I Crossed the Minch' which in 1938 launched the ribaldries of the poem "Bagpipe Music" while recording, though rather discreetly, how MacNeice ran off with the wife of the painter William Coldstream and had liberating sex with her in the black Calvinist houses of the Western Isles at the pit of the 1930s slump: surely deserving a Nobel Prize for libertinism.*[288]

The book includes the much renowned "Bagpipe Music":

> *It's no go my honey love, it's no go my poppet;*

> *Work your hands from day to day, the winds will blow the profit.*

---

287   p99 in M MacIver 1990 **Pilgrim Souls: History of Mary and Hector MacIver** *Aberdeen.*
288   Harvie C 2007 http://www.theguardian.com/commentisfree/2007/oct/09/missinglouismacneice 9 Oct. Accessed 21/8/15.

The glass is falling hour by hour, the glass will fall for ever,

But if you break the bloody glass you won't hold up the weather.

One has to search a little to find what effect Hector MacIver had on '*I Crossed the Minch*' other than being a genial host. One critic picks out where there is clear evidence of MacNeice and MacIver collaborating in an analysis of the difference between a dance in the village of Shawbost, part of the "Celtic timelessness" as they saw it, and a concert in the town of Stornoway – where the dancers were "*becoming objectified, alienated products of the music industry.*"[289]

As MacNeice himself put it in 'I Crossed the Minch' "*... one could thank God that one was not a citizen of Stornoway... European man at his worst*". The point that MacIver and MacNeice seemed to be making was that the entertainment in Shawbost was an indigenous local product; the culture of Stornoway they saw as imported.

One 21st century Hebridean critic has written to me:

> *MacNeice's view of Stornoway. What did he expect?*
> *For centuries the town has been the antithesis of rural Lewis:*
> *anti-Gaelic, weak in religious faith, hedonistic, eager to adopt*
> *imported behavioural trends (e.g. cinema-going, flapper attire in*
> *the late 20s, complex female hairstyles). Cailleachs* [old ladies]
> *from distant townships would actually stop to stare at the latest*
> *outlandish fashions among the gilded urban youth.*[290]

How much Hector appreciated MacNeice's book is sadly unrecorded. This would have been interesting to know, not least because of what is said by one reviewer (in 2007) on the book's re -publication:

> *MacNeice moans about the Island people, the drab landscape,*
> *'the monotony of heather', the food... He gropes his way over the*

289 p73 J Kerrigan 2011 in P Mackay et al (Eds) **Modern Irish and Scottish Poetry** *Cambrid*ge.
290 Personal communication to the author.

islands with his eyes and ears closed. The only conversations he records are with people of standing; the editor of the Stornoway Gazette, which was produced in English, schoolteachers or his middle class friends... The locals he mentions only in passing as a means of providing him hospitality which he appears to accept as his right. The Gaelic language he holds up as a barrier to local conversation.[291]

Between one thing and another, one can understand why the book was as poorly received in Stornoway as it was in the MacIver home in Shawbost.

World War II came; and MacIver joined the Navy. He wrote modestly but eloquently about convoy duties in the North Atlantic. His command of his second language, almost Conrad-like, shines through:

A destroyer, by the very traits of her character, never fails to provide excitement; her movements are unpredictable, her vitality inexhaustible. In the very smoothest of seas, a shiver of life from her engine rooms runs through her whole fabric; she resembles the pulsating body of a greyhound preparing for the chase; and if she decides to turn in her tracks, as she often does, she exercises her narrow circle with the neatness of compass and pencil upon paper.

Anyway, for a whole summer, while we escorted convoys up and down the coast with our ship keeping guard, marshalling the long column of merchant ships and rounding up vagrants, I watched her with interest. I already felt that if, some day, I went back to my profession, I should often be tempted to digress from the strict theme of literature to talk for a moment about destroyers.[292]

And MacIver kept building even in war on his literary contacts, contacts that were to enrich the intellectual and cultural

---

291   M McPartlin 2007 **The New Review.**
292   p107 M MacIver 1990 **Pilgrim Souls: History of Mary and Hector MacIver** *Aberdeen.*

lives of subsequent students, not least Karl Miller. Neil Gunn sent letters to MacIver:

I wrote a book on the herring industry of a century ago 'The Silver Darlings' and it's to be filmed in the north later this year.

As did Chris Grieve (Hugh MacDiarmid):

Sorry my reply is belated. The trouble is that working as an engineer on munitions, I have excessively long hours and practically no time to myself at all... However hard physical work (hitherto unknown to me) has suited me well enough in every other respect, physically, psychologically and pecuniarily [sic] – and I venture to hope that you have a like tale to tell.[293]

One of Hector's naval commanders was Angus, Marquis Graham, later the Duke of Montrose and famous (or infamous) in the 1960s in the rebellious Ian Smith's Rhodesian government. Graham had learned Gaelic at Balliol College in Oxford: where else indeed would a Scottish aristocrat choose to learn Gaelic? He went to the Hebrides on leave with MacIver. There he not only conversed with the locals: he also addressed an assembly of secondary school students in the Nicolson Institute in Gaelic.

Hector was torpedoed twice. On one of these occasions a fellow-officer attempted to repel with an oar his efforts to climb aboard a half-filled lifeboat. However he survived the war.[294]

In 1945 he returned to the Royal High School; and it was then that he as teacher and Karl Miller as school student first encountered each other. One of the other English teachers in the school, Charles McAra, recalled much later:

Hector MacIver became one of the outstanding teachers of English in Scotland in the two decades immediately after the

---

293   p110 M MacIver 1990 **Pilgrim Souls: History of Mary and Hector MacIver** *Aberdeen.*

294   And one night in what was then the (Edinburgh) North British Hotel recognised the fellow officer and assaulted him.

war. This may sound like a very large claim, but its truth can be supported in three ways: by the achievement of his best pupils; by the intellectual stimulus and pleasure he gave to hundreds of boys who had no pretensions as English specialists; and by the way in which through his own example and enthusiasm he taught a large number of young English masters their job and encouraged them to go on to posts of higher responsibility.[295]

Miller himself wrote about Hector in 1971 that:

When I was his pupil at the Royal High School of Edinburgh, Hector used to tell stories about the faculty of second sight, which seemed to be an important matter, still, in the Hebrides where he grew up... To Lowland school-children, Hector came as a revelation: an exile from the Western Isles, from the 'lone shieling of the misty island', he had qualities of dignity, elegance, eloquence and fantasy that seemed not only exotic but literally portentous.[296]

And much later, as recently as 2011, Miller referred in an essay to language and cultural issues that divided Scotland:

Hector MacIver had as much trouble speaking the Scots of Robert Burns as Noël Coward would have had. Highlanders were strange when I was in Edinburgh... My family used to refer to my sophisticated teacher as 'the cheuchter', an ugly word of Gaelic origin which meant a rustic or a hick.[297]

For both MacIver and Miller, these remained lifelong issues. MacIver was a Hebridean but with an identity more firmly rooted in Edinburgh than in either Stornoway or London, yet friends with Norman MacCaig, Sorley Maclean, WH Auden, Louis MacNeice and Dylan Thomas; Miller, a lowland Scot with some Irish ancestry, made his entire career firmly in London but was a close friend of

295   p185 C McAra **Scottish Schoolmasters** in K Miller (Ed) 2008 **Memoirs of a Modern Scotland**, 2nd Edition *London.*
296   pp 94–5 K Miller Romantic Town in K Miller (Ed) 2008 **Memoirs of a Modern Scotland,** 2nd Edition *London.*
297   K Miller 2011 **Tretower to Clyro: Essays** *London.*

Seamus Heaney, of VS Pritchett and of many others.[298]

Karl Miller's debt to his school and to his teacher of English, Hector MacIver, he acknowledged for the rest of his life. Alan Taylor, in his Herald obituary of Karl Miller, speculates on the writers who moulded Miller:[299]

> *It was MacIver who left the greatest impression. "Poetry, for him, was very much a matter of lines, lines to quote, lines to conjure with, and lines to chalk up on the blackboard, lines you could borrow and adapt..." Miller might have* [been] *referring to himself.*

And a Scotsman interview of 2011 records some detail of Miller's school experiences:

> *MacCaig had worn the Royal High uniform ten years before* [Miller] *but they were still friends, thanks largely to Hector MacIver, the head of English at the school and tutor to poets... Miller got to know both MacDiarmid and MacCaig when he was still at school. "They were both kind to me, even MacDiarmid, who was an abrasive person. But Norman was an extraordinary creature. I was struck by the fact that he was capable of standing in the wind and rain outside the main Edinburgh Post Office talking about Lorca with a 16-year-old boy for half an hour. Not many established writers would have done that, but he did. He made a huge impression on me.*[300]

One suspects that the 16-yr-old Karl Miller may also have made a huge impression on MacCaig.

Hector's cultural interests were not narrowly intellectual either:

---

298 Karl Miller, as several of his obituaries pointed out, had tastes that went beyond narrow English literature – an abiding love of football, notably for Tottenham Hotspur and for the football writings of Danny Blanchflower and of Hans Keller.

299 http://www.heraldscotland.com/opinion/obituaries/13181988.Karl_Miller/ Accessed 29/08/2015.

300 Scotsman 2011 http://www.scotsman.com/lifestyle/books/interview-karl-miller-journalist-1-1755599 Accessed 29/08/2015.

Ronnie Corbett, a previous pupil of Hector, also became well known as a comedian. When we were first married I had to listen to every 'Crackerjack' programme with Hector, for he was so interested in following the beginning of Ronnie's successful career.[301]

Corbett and Miller were exact, if unlikely, contemporaries in the Royal High School.

In 1965, Hector took ill. His cat was also ill, as his wife records:

When Hector was dying, Peader was terminally ill also, and Hector said to the tiger-striped Peader as she lay on the quilt on Hector's bed – 'Ah, little one, we're both on the way out'.[302]

In early 1966 Karl Miller visited for the last time the teacher and mentor he had acquired some 20 years earlier.

On 30 April 1966, Hector MacIver died. He was 55 years old.

301 p192–3 in M MacIver 1990 **Pilgrim Souls: History of Mary and Hector MacIver** *Aberdeen.*
302 p149 in M MacIver 1990 **Pilgrim Souls: History of Mary and Hector MacIver** *Aberdeen.*

11

CONCLUSIONS

Back in the second half of the 19th century, the pupil teacher system in elementary schools, the associated income stream for the pupil teachers and the "Queen's scholarships" which sent the best of the pupil teachers for college training provided an important route to teacher qualification. Increasingly it was used by women, as we have seen in Chapters 2 and 4: indeed, until the 1890s, it was their only route to a higher education qualification. The scheme operated in broadly similar ways in Scotland and in England.

However the development of widespread (and largely free) secondary education in Scotland (1885–1910) was well ahead of what happened in England. Perversely it was less contentious and therefore faster, as we have seen, in the then parishes of Govan and of Stornoway than in the parishes of Glasgow and of Edinburgh.[303] The university age participation rate, as we shall see, was much higher in Scotland than in England.

The Scottish university system expanded in the period 1895 to 1913 having been largely static for 20 years before that. The initiation of female graduation (from 1892) and the foundation of the Carnegie Trust for the Universities of Scotland (1901) played a large part in the expansion.

The extent to which education is a gateway to social mobility then or now can be overstated. For Donald Mackenzie, John Munro and Murdo Murray it certainly was; for John L Robertson, Donald Maclean, Robert M MacIver and Hector MacIver it was perhaps more a reinforcement of what their parents had already achieved by one means or another, albeit for them a platform for further advances.[304]

In other words, in the late 19th and early 20th century and now, the extent to which education was and is a route to social mobility is problematic. For some it was and is; for others it was and is more

---

303 With boundaries hugely different to those of the 21st century – insofar as the concept of "parish" survives at all. But one gets the general idea.

304 For relevant historical data see pp 294–335 RD Anderson 1983 **Education & Opportunity in Victorian Scotland** *Edinburgh.*

a confirmation of an upward mobility which an earlier generation of their family had already managed, sometimes through educational mechanisms but often through other means e.g. mercantile success. This has been variously dubbed "elite recruitment" to use Anderson's words of the 1980s; and the "glass floor" to use words of the 2010s.[305]

We can illustrate that by the difference between two British prime ministers.

J Ramsay Macdonald came from a very poor background in a single parent family and was educated in an elementary school in Lossiemouth. There he distinguished himself academically in a way that eventually led to No 10 Downing St. His social mobility was (largely) educationally powered and in his own generation.[306]

Harold Macmillan had a crofter great grandfather of poor Arran origins whose son founded the great publishing house of Macmillans.[307] Harold was educated at Eton and Cambridge; and married a daughter of the Duke of Devonshire. The most decisive upward social mobility of the Arran crofting family was achieved two generations earlier by his grandfather, and Harold's education was in essence but confirmation of that, although also a springboard to political success. That is the "glass floor" idea.

Incidentally Ramsay Macdonald was intensely ashamed of his starting point in life and sought to conceal it. Harold Macmillan in a quite different way was equally deceitful. When it suited him, he boasted of having come from a poor crofting family.

'Rab' Butler allegedly said in 1975:

How was Harold Macmillan when you met him? Was he the Duke's son-in-law or the crofter's great grand-son?[308]

Macmillan was not the last UK prime minister to behave in that way. Not even of those called Harold.

---

305   A McKnight 2015 https://www.gov.uk/government/uploads/system/uploads/ attachment_data/file/447575/Downward_mobility_opportunity_hoarding_and_the_glass_ floor.pdf.

306   See page 10.

307   p10 DR Thorpe 2010 **Supermac: The life of Harold Macmillan** *London*.

308   p9 DR Thorpe 2010 **Supermac: The life of Harold Macmillan** *London*.

We have told the stories, albeit one very briefly, of three school students of the first decade of the 20th century who came from impeccably working class origins: Mackenzie, Munro and Murray – two the sons of crofting/fishing families and one the son of a crofter/shoemaker.

Were they typical? That would be too strong a claim. But we think they epitomise some trends in that 1900s decade.

Chapter 4 has provided evidence of four overlapping and mutually reinforcing developments in Scotland:

> "higher grade" secondary schooling had continued to expand;

> bursaries to attend secondary schools were now common, if small; and the same was true of bursaries for attendance at universities;

> universities, after two decades of little growth, were expanding; and

> by as early as 1904 half of all Scottish university undergraduates were having their tuition fees paid by the Carnegie Trust for the Universities of Scotland.[309]

Some sons (and indeed by then some daughters) of fishermen and shoemakers had found sources of support. But we should be careful about exaggeration: the commonest beneficiaries, as we have already noted, appear to have been the children of the skilled working class and of the lower middle class.[310]

The expansion of free secondary education and wider provision of secondary school bursaries and of university bursaries certainly benefitted boys and girls of working class origins in the early years of the 20th century **in absolute terms** i.e. numbers rose. However, **in relative terms**, the numbers of

---

309   Not to be confused with other Carnegie Trusts e.g. the one that created the Carnegie and Haldane hostels in Stornoway in the 1920s.

310   The definitive work on this, as we have noted earlier, is RD Anderson 1983 **Education & Opportunity in Victorian Scotland** *Edinburgh.*

boys and girls of middle class origins who benefitted rose at least equally quickly. That pattern has prevailed right through into the 21st century; and remains in 2017 a current topic of debate.

Why were these developments, although broadly Scotland-wide, so well exemplified in the Island of Lewis?

Lewis (and notably the Parish of Stornoway) was in the mid to late 19th century the most populous area of the Highlands and Islands (and possibly of rural Scotland) without a "higher" (i.e. secondary) school.[311] Inverness and its hinterland were more populous; but Inverness had its Royal Academy, founded back in the 17th century. So the need was more obvious in Lewis than in most areas of rural Scotland.

If the problem was obvious, there were at least some elements of the solution that were also reasonably obvious, at least to people of the calibre of JL Robertson and WJ Gibson.

In the late 19th century parish of Stornoway, even in some parts of its "landward" i.e. rural area, many children could manage a daily commute to the Nicolson School or, in the more far-flung parts of the "landward" areas of the parish of Stornoway and in the other school board parishes of the Island i.e. Barvas, Uig, Carloway and Lochs, a weekly commute to lodgings in the town of Stornoway[312] (even though the commute was usually achieved by walking or by cart). Travel for aspirant scholars in the Inner Hebrides or Orkney or Shetland or the southern isles of the Outer Hebrides was much more problematic because of sea journeys or, in some of the mainland Highlands, because of much longer land mileages.

So the "Stornoway solution", if we can call it that, was followed, sometimes quickly and sometimes slowly, in some other parts of the Highlands and Islands e.g. in Portree in 1906. But the logistics elsewhere were often more challenging: even today in the 21st century, the 12 year-old scholars from the Ross of Mull

---

311 My acknowledgements to Professor James Hunter who first led me to think about 19th century population statistics in different parts of the Highlands and Islands.
312 p158 D Macdonald 1978 **Lewis: A History of the Island** *Edinburgh.*

can face a 30-mile bus journey to Craignure early on a Monday morning, a ferry to Oban, four nights in a school hostel in Oban and the reverse journey on a Friday evening.

There was a demand from middle class aspirant parents (e.g. the parents of Robert M MacIver and Donald Maclean) for an isles-based route to university for their children; and quickly from some working class families as well (e.g. the families of Donald Mackenzie, of John Munro and of Murdo Murray).

While these families faced both direct financial costs in schooling their children beyond the age of 13 or 14 and the "opportunity costs" of keeping teenagers away from fishing and crofting, the introduction of new school and university bursaries (from 1895) and of university Carnegie scholarships (from 1901) helped.[313]

JL Robertson, who was to become the Senior Chief Inspector of Schools for all of Scotland in 1911, was someone of high ability. And he was a shrewd, if unsentimental, person manager. It was he *de facto* who dismissed Forbes in 1893 and replaced him with WJ Gibson; and, as we have seen in Chapter 2, in the 1910s he exiled someone whom he perceived as an underperforming rural Lewis headteacher to being head teacher in Scarp, roughly the Hebridean equivalent of running a small Siberian power station.

Scotch[314] Education Department reports for the years of 1910–11, 1912–13, and 1913–1914 extolled what had happened in developing secondary education in Lewis as a prime example of the superlative nature of Scotch Education Department policy

---

313   It took until the Anderson Committee Report of 1960 for the UK government to introduce almost universal payment of university tuition fees and means-tested student maintenance allowances both in England and in Scotland. This system lasted, broadly untouched, until about 1990; but with the value of the student maintenance allowance (high for students of the mid-1960s) eroded over three decades by sub-inflationary rises. From 1990 successive governments, of various political hues, incrementally dismantled the system of maintenance allowances. It is a complicated story. The story of the size of university tuition fees and of who paid, and pays them, is even more complex. See http://www.historyandpolicy.org/policy-papers/papers/going-to-university-funding-costs-benefits Accessed 20 July 2016.

314   As it was until 1918. "Scottish Education Department" for many decades after that.

and an example to be copied elsewhere in Scotland.[315] Now,
even if Robertson and Gibson were influential in the thinking
of Sir John Struthers,[316] the author of these reports, the reality
did represent much progress since the unsteady "secondary
school" Nicolson years of the very early 1890s.

An even greater, if exaggerated, tribute came in the House
of Lords in 1916.

It is by Viscount Haldane and is recorded to this day in
the (now digitised) Hansard for the House of Lords of 12 July
1916. RB Haldane (1856–1928), a graduate of the universities
of Edinburgh and of Göttingen, was in the UK cabinet as
Secretary of State for War 1905–1912; and as Lord Chancellor
1912–1915. He was a noted expert on education; and was highly
critical of education at the time in England, comparing it
unfavourably with Welsh education, with Scottish education
and with German education. (That last sentiment cost him his
cabinet post in 1915. There was a Great War raging – against
Germany.)[317]

Haldane said:

> There have been great advances in other parts of the country...
> I have already alluded to the steps forward which have
> been made in Scotland. I should like to go to one concrete
> illustration about the effect of the reform of education in
> Scotland.

> The Hebrides is a congested area, thickly populated by crofters
> who previously were able to provide but little education
> for their children. Then there came compulsory elementary
> education, and the sons of the crofters used to go to school;

---

315   p242 RD Anderson 1983 **Education & Opportunity in Victorian Scotland**
Edinburgh.

316   Secretary of the Scotch Education Department i.e. its top civil servant. He was
the second such one, succeeding Henry Craik. He himself had ascended to power from
lowly beginnings as a pupil teacher. However it was he who abolished the system of
pupil teachers – in 1906.

317   pp307–308 M Bostridge 2014 **The Fateful Year: England 1914** *London.*

but after school was over there was no provision for them under the Education Endowments Act.[318]

What was called the Nicolson Institute at Stornoway was turned into a secondary school, and the effect upon the Hebrides has been extraordinary. The sons and daughters of the crofters go there, many of them with little bursaries which they get through the county council. They get a secondary school education at the Nicolson Institute, and from there they go out into the world to become teachers, doctors, lawyers, and ministers; the effect also on the social life of the Hebrides has been very remarkable.

I give your Lordships that as an illustration of what reform will do if it is judicially and simply applied.[319]

Some of this overstates both the short-term and the longer-term effects of the 1872 Education (Scotland) Act on the Island of Lewis. But is certainly a counter-weight to the judgment of (the normally incisive and convincing) John Macleod: *"The 1872 Act did, in fact, very little for Lewis."*[320]

Haldane went on the following year to expand his argument in a book chapter:

In Scotland the Education Act passed still more recently in 1908 has carried the process a stage further, with the result that instruction of a secondary type is more widely provided than it is south of the Tweed.[321]

Some of the statistics in the 1917 Haldane chapter are

318   The Act that had reformed the pre-existing endowed schools. What Haldane was pointing out, in a manner now slightly obscure, was that the Island of Lewis had lacked any school equivalent to Inverness Royal Academy or to Aberdeen Grammar School or to Montrose Academy.
319   The full speech can be viewed at http://hansard.millbanksystems.com/lords/1916/jul/12/training-of-the-nation Accessed 20th July 2016.
320   p202 J Macleod 2010 **None Dare Oppose** *Edinburgh*. Although Macleod was focusing on Gaelic-medium education in his remarks.
321   p80 R Haldane '*National Education*', Chapter V in Lord Cromer et al 1917 **After War Problems** *London*.

illuminating. In England, 39% of 13–16 yr-olds got no education. The comparable figure in Scotland was 28%. The university participation rate of 16–25 yr-olds in England was 3 per 1000; in Scotland it was almost 10 per 1000.

The key differences between Scotland and England in fact long predated the 1908 Act to which Haldane refers. As we have seen the development of Board-provided secondary education was well in flow in Stornoway by the early 1890s and earlier in areas such as Govan. In England such action by Boards was deemed illegal (by the Cockerton judgment[322]) until an Education Act of 1902 enabled new education authorities both to establish their own secondary schools and provide funds to existing endowed schools. The English solution was similar to the Scottish one, but years later.

Let us move on from schools to further education and to higher education. For, if direct access to the four ancient universities from a reasonably local school became moderately common from 1900 onwards and accelerated with the ever-expanding provision of university tuition fee scholarships in the early decades of the 20th century, the story of further education (or, for that matter, of wider higher education) provision is geographically much more uneven across Scotland.

Modern further education provision is largely a story of the years after 1945;[323] and the growth of further education colleges in Scotland's major cities was rapid, even dramatic – but largely only in cities.

The development of further education in rural Scotland was very uneven and generally slow. Skye did not acquire a college offering further education qualifications until Sabhal Mor Ostaig started such provision in 1983; Argyllshire had very meagre

---

322   RS Betts 1992 *'In Limbo: Edward Hance and the Cockerton Judgement 1901'* **Journal of Educational Administration and History** 24:1.
323   Although Stow College was explicitly founded as an FE college in Glasgow in 1935. And various institutions operating in what we would now call "further education" had been around for longer than that.

provision until the establishment of Argyll College in 1997; and the stories in Orkney and in Shetland were very similar.

In Stornoway some people met in a room in Stornoway in 1950. They had a dilemma that most of us will never face.

They were part-owners, amidst thousands of others, of a castle i.e. a castle which had been bequeathed by Lord Leverhulme in the 1920s to a local community trust. They were unsure in 1950 what do with their castle. It was a castle with a controversial past: having been built by Sir James Matheson in the 19th century. He was recently described on a poster outside the castle itself as "an astute trader". That, I suppose, is indeed one way of describing the biggest and most notorious drug-dealer of the 19th century: for he was responsible for importing vast quantities of opium from India into China. This was a man who, with his business partner Jardine, induced the British government to declare war on China to keep his trade going.[324, 325]

The people at the 1950 meeting eventually reached a conclusion: to make the castle a place of learning. And that is how Lews Castle College UHI, now part of the University of the Highlands and Islands, began. Wise people these four were; and their advice was significant in persuading the Stornoway Trust and Ross & Cromarty Education Authority to establish the college. Out of a building financed from the fruits of infamy, they created an institution for good.

The decision to create a Lews Castle College in 1953 with its nine staff and its 83 students was therefore for its time far-sighted, and a most unusual one for a rural area.

So, what has changed in school education and in further and higher education in Lewis and more generally in the Highlands and Islands over the last 50 or even 100 years? There are perhaps three points to be made:

---

324   Chapter 12 RJ Grace 2014 **Opium and Empire the lives and careers of William Jardine and James Matheson** *Montreal.*
325   Chapter 6 T Hunt 2014 **10 Cities that Made an Empire** *London.*

Firstly, we observe that 100 years ago, as the story of Robert M MacIver (and of many others) shows, formal education often led to migration and emigration rather than in any way being about local civic and community development (that is the James Hunter thesis which we describe in our introduction); and 50 years ago this was true of much of the further education at the Lews Castle College. This is now less true. Much of the curriculum of Lews Castle College, of Inverness College, of North Highland College, of Argyll College and so on (constituent but semi-autonomous parts of the University of the Highlands and Islands) is not a pre-career prelude to migration but early and mid-career capacity-building for those already in local employment.

Secondly, the topic of university or, more generally, of higher education is more complex. University education in the 1900s for Hebrideans and mainland highlanders meant (page 63, Chapter 4) Aberdeen, Edinburgh or Glasgow universities. For many Highland and Islands students e.g. Alexander Macdonald, Robert M MacIver, Donald Maclean, Donald Mackenzie, Murdo Murray and Hector MacIver, it led as Professor Hunter noted to careers outside Lewis or even outside Scotland. But, even from quite early in the 20th century, as the Haldane speech illustrates, although perhaps with a degree of exaggeration, there were graduate opportunities in the Lewis labour market and we have seen examples both in Chapter 4 and in Chapter 5 of locals who returned to these. And what became Colleges of Education, through their two-year and then three-year diploma courses, opened opportunities (generally, but not exclusively, for girls) to attend mainland colleges and in many cases to return to island careers.

Thirdly higher education traditionally meant going to study, usually full-time, at a non-Highland location. In the 19th and 20th century, it was generally only urban students who could access higher education locally and who could choose between doing so on a part-time or a full-time basis. The advent of the Open University in 1971, of what has now become the University of the Highlands and Islands in the 1990s and of on-line learning opportunities (from a variety of providers, but notably from the Open University and the University of the Highlands and Islands) has changed that somewhat.[326]

In this book, I with some pals set out, as I said at the start,

to provide some historical analysis;

and to tell some stories.

It is for others to judge the analysis. Much of it has been done before. I have simply tried to make the analysis more readable and more accessible, largely through illustrative stories. I have tagged to that, as Sir Tom Devine advocates, a caution about the atypicality of some of the stories and the connection of atypicality to myth-making.

Stories perhaps most affect the story-teller more than the readers of the stories. To this day, a century after one died and some 75 years after the death of the other, it is the poignant tales of John Munro of Aignish and of Murdo Macdonald of Crola which resonate most with this story-teller. They had rather austere theological beliefs. John Munro would not have thought himself a saint. Murdo Crola would not have thought himself a saint. But they were both remarkable and inspirational people.

For more than half a century, I have revered them.

---

326   For an extended treatment of this, see F Rennie 2005 **Distributed Learning in the Western Isles** at www.lews.uhi.ac.uk/research-enterprise/contact/prof-frank-rennie/ eLearningWI.pdf Accessed 6/3/2017.

SELECT BIBLIOGRAPHY

Anderson RD 1983 **Education & Opportunity in Victorian Scotland** *Edinburgh*

Bone TR 1968 **School Inspection in Scotland 1840–1966** *Edinburgh*

Cruickshank M 1970 **History of the Training of Teachers in Scotland** *London*

Devine TM 2011 **To The Ends of the Earth** *London*

Devine TM 2012 **The Scottish Nation: A Modern History** *London*

Grace RG 2014 **Opium and Empire: the lives and careers of William Jardine and James Matheson** *Montreal*

Hunter J 1999 **Last of the Free: A History of the Highlands and Islands of Scotland** *Edinburgh*

Hunter J 2000 **The Making of the Crofting Community (New Edition)** *Edinburgh*

Hutchinson R 2003 **The Soap Man: Lewis, Harris and Lord Leverhulme** *Edinburgh*

Macdonald D 1978 **Lewis: A History of the Island** *Edinburgh*

MacIver RM 1968 **As a Tale That Is Told** *Chicago*

Macleod J 2009 **When I Heard the Bell** *Edinburgh*

Miller K (Ed) 2008 **Memoirs of a Modern Scotland, 2nd Edition** *London*

Smith C 2001 **Around the Peat-Fire** *Edinburgh*